SPORTS ★★★★★★★★★★★
SUPERSTARS
FROM BLACK HISTORY
★★★★★★★★★★★★★★★★★★★★★★

SPORTS ★★★★★★★★★★★ SUPERSTARS FROM BLACK HISTORY

★★★★★★★★★★★★★★★★★★★★★★★★★

Inspiring Stories from the Amazing Careers of
★ SERENA WILLIAMS ★ SIMONE BILES ★
★ ALLYSON FELIX ★ LEBRON JAMES ★
and Many More African American Sports Legends

SOPHIA MURPHY

ULYSSES BOOKS
FOR YOUNG READERS

Published by:
Ulysses Books for Young Readers
an imprint of Ulysses Press
PO Box 3440
Berkeley, CA 94703
www.ulyssespress.com

ISBN: 978-1-64604-7-192
Library of Congress Control Number: 2024934552

Printed in the United States
10 9 8 7 6 5 4 3 2 1

Front cover design: Lindsey Bailey
Project editor: Renee Rutledge
Copyeditor: Sherian Brown
Production: Winnie Liu

To my two boys, Andre and Aaron: may you live big, beautiful lives and follow your wildest dreams. And to Wayne, who always supported mine.

CONTENTS

INTRODUCTION

You may be young, but you've already got big dreams.

Maybe you want to be a better student or athlete. Or maybe you're thinking ahead and aspire to be the best at whatever you do later in life. Whether your dreams are far off in the future or something you're working on right now, it's okay to wonder how to turn them into reality. Sometimes, all you need is a little inspiration. This book is full of inspirational stories about iconic Black athletes of today and the past who pursued their dreams and made them a reality.

If you're familiar with names like Serena Williams, LeBron James, or Simone Biles, then you already know they are the best in the world at what they do. But how did they get there? What motivated them? What are their greatest achievements?

Those athletes may seem untouchable now, but did you know they were once like you? Just kids with a world of possibilities before them, trying to figure it all out. They had families, friends, problems, and worries like everyone else. But they also had an unstoppable dream.

This book will answer some of the questions you have about your favorite athletes. But it will also introduce you to other legendary Black athletes from the past who dreamed the impossible dream in the face of the hardest challenges.

We've come a long way from a time of segregation in the US, when Black people weren't granted the same rights as white Americans. That inequality spread through all areas of American society, even sports. Where we are today rests solely on the shoulders of the Black sportsmen and women who fought for the inclusion of Black athletes in professional sports. These pioneers of recent history were the first to desegregate national teams, win Olympic gold, and set first-time records. They bore the brunt of racism while forever changing the face of the sports they played. It couldn't have been easy, but they did it and, in so doing, changed a nation.

The same strength, resilience, and drive we admire in today's Black athletes was abundant in those who've gone before. Sometimes, it's easy to forget that someone had to be the first. But in this book, we'll celebrate those firsts who made it possible for others to reach higher heights and set new standards.

Striving for your dreams can often be filled with pitfalls and set-backs, but the end is always worth the struggle. There's so much to learn from these inspirational stories. And the biggest lesson is that what you do in between the dream and the reality makes it all possible.

The life stories of these great athletes will inspire you to dream big and keep reaching for your goals, even when times are hard, even when you're unsure of yourself. Because when you believe in yourself and work toward those dreams, whatever they may be, you'll find you can do anything.

CHAPTER 1

TENNIS

SERENA WILLIAMS AND ALTHEA GIBSON

SERENA WILLIAMS

....

"Whatever path you decide to take in the future and whether it's tennis or some other field, I want you to remember this: You have to believe in yourself when no one else does. When I was growing up I went on the court with just a ball, racquet, hope, and a dream."[1]

....

EARLY YEARS

You know the name Serena Williams, but how exactly did the youngest of five girls become the biggest name in tennis? Determination, hard work, and a desire to be the best played a considerable part. But for Serena, winner of twenty-three Grand Slam singles titles, it all began by believing that she could.

Serena Williams's story is as unique as yours. After all, we all have our own stories to tell. And those stories make us who we are. No great athlete wakes up one day and is suddenly at the top of their game. There are highs and lows, good times and bad, and in between, a whole lot of practice and hard work.

Born to Oracene Price, a nurse, and Richard Williams, a security firm owner, in 1981, Serena was just a baby when her family moved

---

[1] Mahalakshmi Murali, "'You Have to Believe in Yourself When No One Else Does'—Serena Williams Addresses Class of 2020 at Mouratoglou's Academy," Essentially Sports, July 7, 2020, https://www.essentiallysports.com /tennis-news-wta-you-have-to-believe-in-yourself-when-no-one-else-does -serena-williams-addresses-class-of-2020-at-mouratoglous-academy.

from Saginaw, Michigan, to Compton, California. Compton was a rough neighborhood known for gang violence, crime, and hard living. But that rough upbringing was exactly what Richard Williams sought for his daughters. While it sounds strange, this key decision would set his children on a path to greatness. You see, he wanted his daughters to face adversity, experience tough times, and come out the better for it. Serena's parents had four other children—all girls. Serena was the youngest, and Venus was fifteen months older. Serena's oldest sisters were Yetunde, Lyndrea, and Isha.

Richard Williams was many things: a hardworking father, a family man, and a visionary. When he moved his family to Compton, he did so with the future of his daughters in mind. He hoped to set his children up for success in whatever they chose to do and ensure they could handle anything that came their way. But he also had a plan.

A TV program gave him the idea to change the course of life for his family. While watching the televised French Open (a major tennis tournament) in 1978, he realized the opportunities afforded to those players, and he wanted the same opportunities for his children. So he set about getting it. He and his wife taught themselves tennis and then introduced it to the girls. Tennis became a way of life for the Williams family, and it was always a family affair, with both of Serena's parents involved in training all their children.

But the courts in Compton didn't lend themselves to world-class status. They played in less-than-perfect conditions on the two run-down, neglected courts in Serena's neighborhood. But they played nonetheless. Richard Williams and his family made it work. He often took the kids from neighborhood to neighborhood in his van so they could experience playing at different locations and on different courts. And even when those courts were as dilapidated as the ones in their own neighborhood, the girls played and played and played.

As a kid, Serena loved the time she spent with her family. When she was a toddler, she'd watch her sisters play, but when she turned three, her father gave her a tennis racquet and set the wheels in motion.

Serena grew up in a loving and tight-knit family. And while her parents could be strict and disciplined, they also taught the girls to work as a unit and to support and help each other. The sisters were very close throughout their lives. Serena was closest in age to Venus. And much of Serena's story is intertwined with Venus's, a world-renowned, record-breaking tennis star in her own right. And because of tennis and their path as professional tennis players, Venus and Serena's connection would be made even stronger.

All five sisters practiced every day—sometimes before school, sometimes after school, and whenever they could get it in. And while all the sisters were decent players, it soon became apparent that Venus and Serena had something special. As the older sister, Venus was the first to stand out, though Serena would eventually catch up to and surpass her sister. But that would come much later.

The sisters didn't feel burdened by all the tennis practice because this was what they knew. And Richard Williams wasn't a harsh taskmaster. It was important to him that the girls have fun while practicing on the courts, improving their skills, and gaining the confidence they needed to succeed. He often posted motivational signs around the tennis courts so the girls could read them as they played. This was something Serena would later copy on a smaller scale when she got older. During her tournaments, she kept journals, her "matchbooks," as she called them. They were full of motivational notes, observations, and entries. She would also post motivational sticky notes on her racquet bag and read them repeatedly during breaks or when switching sides.

Richard Williams made sure his daughters had access to many opportunities. And two of those opportunities became defining moments for Serena. Her first was a tennis clinic run by Billie Jean King, a world-famous tennis star. Seven-year-old Serena was excited about the clinic and saw it as an opportunity to show off her stuff. She thought she would be a standout among the other young players and thereby catch the attention of King. But unfortunately, she didn't play well and cried when Venus did better than she did. While the day didn't go how she wanted it to, she learned that it's okay if things don't work out as planned. This lesson would help carry her through other difficult times.

Her other defining moment came when she was eight years old. As Venus's star rose, Serena was seen as a tagalong. She was always happy for her sister's wins, even when they were adults. But like any younger sibling, Serena wanted to do everything her big sister did. That's how she ended up entering herself into her first recreational tournament. No one other than little Serena knew she had mailed off the entrance form to a tournament Venus was already signed up for. On the tournament day, her parents were shocked to find out Serena was registered. Maybe they were amused at her boldness, or maybe they wanted to see how far she could go, but either way, they let her play. Serena was delighted. And she surprised them even more by winning all her matches; that is, until she was in the finals against Venus. She lost against her sister but won the silver trophy. From then on, her parents and many others saw Serena was as much of a contender as Venus.

When Serena was nine, her family made another move—this time to West Palm Beach, Florida, where acclaimed tennis coach Rick

Macci would train her and Venus at his tennis academy, the Rick Macci Tennis Academy. Macci was a strong influence on their careers and helped them hone their skills. The sisters trained at the academy for upwards of six hours a day. During their time in Florida, the Williams girls, like other kids their age, were also actively involved in activities such as ballet, gymnastics, and karate. But for Serena, nothing held a candle to tennis.

PATH TO SUCCESS

The Williams family, improving on the fundamentals of the game, stayed at the academy for four years. During that time, the girls didn't play any junior tournaments. This was an unusual move by Richard Williams and Macci, as playing in the junior circuits was commonly done before entering the major tournaments. But their father kept the girls away from the pressures of the circuit so they could stay interested in the game. He didn't want them to burn out from tennis at an early age, as he had seen happen to other young players. Instead he wanted to foster a real love for the art of the game. But soon enough, they would make their debut.

In 1995, Serena made her professional tournament debut at the Bell Challenge in Quebec City. She was fourteen years old and still young, and maybe her age played a part in the outcome. It wasn't the debut she imagined it would be. She lost her match. But this was when she also began to understand that winning was up to her. She'd have to earn it and fight for it. No one was going to do it for her. She didn't play another tournament until March 1997 at Indian Wells, California, using the time to train, mature, and improve her game.

When she reemerged, it was with the drive and athleticism of a true athlete. She won her first professional doubles title in 1998 at Oklahoma City with Venus. How fitting that she would win the doubles tournament with her sister Venus by her side. Together, they won the gold and began an epic story that would endure their entire professional careers, playing as each other's greatest rival and partner.

From that day forward, the eyes of the tennis world and the media would be on Serena. Winning or losing, she brought attention and excitement to the game and herself wherever she went.

In 2000, Serena and Venus won the Olympic gold medal for women's doubles in tennis. It was Serena's first Olympic medal. It was a momentous occasion and a source of pride for the sisters, though they would go on to win others.

And then there was the "Serena Slam." Imagine having something named after you because you were the best to do it. Well, that was the case here.

So, what's a Serena Slam? In tennis, four major tournaments, also known as Grand Slams (the French Open, Wimbledon, US Open, and the Australian Open) are played throughout the year. Winning one of these is a big deal; winning all four is incredible. Serena was twenty-one and twenty-two when she achieved her first Serena Slam in 1999 and 2000, winning all four Grand Slam titles, though not in the same season. Hence, a new tennis term was coined.

TRIALS AND TRIBULATIONS

Serena's life wasn't without heartbreak. Her golden career has also had some major setbacks and hardships. But it was within those times she found her greatest strength.

The first major test of her fortitude came when she played the Indian Wells Open in 2001. Here, she came face to face with racial prejudice and injustice, and it would shape her game moving forward.

Serena was scheduled to play a semifinal match against her sister Venus, but Venus withdrew due to an injury. Rumors of cheating swirled around the Williams family, and the crowd was angry and unsympathetic. The crowd booed and jeered at Serena as she played in the finals, slinging racist comments while applauding her opponent. The taunts continued for the entire match. It blew her concentration, but more than this, it was shocking and deeply hurtful.

But Serena found strength from deep within and recalled the story of Althea Gibson. Gibson, another great tennis player from the 1950s, endured much racism during her career. Serena told herself she needed to be tough. She thought, "If Althea Gibson could fight her way through much worse, she had an obligation to fight through this."[2] And she did. While Serena ended up winning the game, she and Venus wouldn't play Indian Wells for another fourteen years in protest against the treatment of her family and to call attention to the racism that was pervasive in the sport.

Serena, like many athletes, suffered throughout her career with physical injuries. From knee surgery to back pain, she has experienced it all. She was even diagnosed with blood clots in her legs in 2011. Sometimes, she played through those injuries, and sometimes, they kept her out of the game.

During one of her rehabilitation periods for an injured knee, her oldest sister, Yetunde, died. Serena was adrift after her sister's death and fell into a depression that would keep her from playing for many months. But a goodwill mission to Africa in 2006 helped

---

2 Serena Williams and Daniel Paisner, *Queen of the Court* (New York: Simon & Schuster, 2009).

her overcome her depression. She felt a connection and responsibility to her heritage that changed how she saw herself and her game. When she returned to the sport, it was with a vengeance and a renewed confidence in her abilities.

During the time away from the sport, her tennis ranking slipped. She had dropped to No. 139, far from when she had left at No. 10. She had a long way to go before reaching the top again.

But she fought hard and battled back. A pivotal point in Serena's career came in 2007 at the Australian Open. She entered the tournament ranked only at No. 89; no one expected her to win. She was under a lot of pressure from her sponsors and the focus of much body shaming and negativity from the media. Serena herself didn't expect to win.

She had to play against six top players to make it to the finals, which seemed impossible given her time away from the court and her ranking. But like always, Serena gave it 100 percent, even playing with an injury. Each round, she gained more confidence as she played. She would later say, "The real push came from taking all those negatives and mashing them together into a great big positive. I put it in my head that I would not be beaten down. By my critics. By my peers. By my sponsors. By my opponents."[3] Sheer willpower helped Serena triumph over adversity, and despite the negative press, the pressure she felt, and the physical pain her body was experiencing, she won. She overtook top-ranked Maria Sharapova in the finals, beating her 6-1, 6-2.

With a renewed sense of purpose and a focus on Grand Slams, she went from being a great player to the stuff of legends. She shifted her mindset and focused on winning all the major tournaments.

---

3 Williams and Paisner, *Queen of the Court.*

And that she did, over the years, accumulating title after title and breaking records as she played.

In 2017, after giving birth to her first child, Serena experienced a life-threatening medical emergency. Thankfully, she recovered and used her experience to champion the rights of mothers and babies.

ACHIEVEMENTS

So now that you know a little more about Serena's life, let's get to her extraordinary accomplishments and what made her the icon she is today.

With seventy-three career titles, Serena established herself as one of the most powerful players ever to play tennis. Serena is a celebrated icon in the world of tennis, and her name can be found at the top of every ranking as one of the best players in the game's history.

Serena broke numerous records and collected many titles in her long-standing career. She has won twenty-three Grand Slam titles, the most of any female player in the modern era of the sport.

And with her sister Venus by her side, Serena also won fourteen Grand Slam doubles tournaments, three of which were Olympic wins. Aside from the Olympic gold medals she won with Venus, she also won gold for women's singles at the 2012 London Olympics.

Serena has also attained the very rare Golden Slam title—all four majors combined with an Olympic win. She is only the second woman to have ever done this. The first was Steffi Graf in 1988.

Serena accomplished her namesake Serena Slam twice, first in the 2002/2003 season and again in the 2014/2015 season.

Over the span of her career, she was ranked No. 1 for a whopping 319 weeks, including 186 weeks in a row at the height of her career. In total, she has won a record-setting 367 matches.

Serena's last Grand Slam win was in 2017 against her sister Venus.

LIFE LESSONS

Serena's athletic prowess, powerful serves, and never-back-down philosophy have made her a star and a legend in her time. But what we can learn from Serena's story is more than just how to win but how to thrive in any situation.

In a sport that lacked diversity and minority representation, Serena made a name for herself and her family. And her story couldn't be told without speaking on the tremendous influence of her family. With their support, Serena was able to achieve incredible things. But it was her own drive and determination that became the fuel she needed to keep her dream alive.

What she's shown is a winning mentality can be cultivated and shaped to help you achieve whatever you want in life. Do what you love, take your time and learn, dig deep within yourself for motivation, and believe in yourself even when others don't. These are the things that Serena did to create her winning mentality, and you can, too.

From 1995 to 2022, Serena has been a force in professional tennis. And what a monumental career she's had. The imprint she has left on tennis will be long-lasting. From Naomi Osaka to Coco Gauff, contemporary Black players credit Serena as their childhood influence. And seeing another Black woman dominate the sport factored into their decision to pick up a racquet.

Serena announced in 2022 that she would retire from tennis. At her last match, held at the 2022 US Open, Serena received a standing ovation from fans as she waved a tearful goodbye to a crowded stadium. In her post interview, when asked what she hoped to be remembered by, she said, "I really brought something and bring something to tennis."[4] She was right on that count. There has never been a player like Serena, and she leaves behind a legacy that will stand the test of time. Will there be another Serena? Could it be you? We'll have to wait and see.

4 US Open Tennis Championships, "Serena Williams Press Conference | 2022 US Open Round 3," YouTube, September 3, 2022, https://www.youtube.com /watch?v=abJFrMOyqPM.

ALTHEA GIBSON

....
"I always wanted to be somebody. If I made it, it's half because I was game enough to take a lot of punishment along the way and half because there were a lot of people who cared enough to help me."[5]
....

EARLY YEARS

Sometimes, life can seem like it's all laid out for you, as with Serena Williams, who held her first tennis racquet at the age of three. And other times, it might seem like you've stumbled into it. Certain events and people may appear on your path at just the right time and ultimately change the course of your life. That's what happened to Althea Gibson, the first African American to win a Grand Slam tennis tournament, among many other achievements.

A self-described "wild child," Althea was a rule breaker and misfit who seemed unlikely to take the world by storm, but that's exactly what she did.

Althea was born on August 25, 1927, in the small town of Silver, South Carolina. She grew up in a time in America when segregation, the laws that divided Black and white people, were legal in the South. Her parents, Daniel and Annie Bell Gibson, sharecroppers on a cotton farm, were eager to leave the repression of the Deep South. They set their sights on New York. Though the rest of the country still struggled with racial inequalities and tension,

---

5 Althea Gibson, Edward E. Fitzgerald, and Stephen M. Joseph, *I Always Wanted to Be Somebody* (New York: Noble and Noble, 1970).

segregation didn't exist in the northern states, and many Black people migrated north in search of prosperity and new beginnings.

When Althea's parents made the move, she was just three years old and their only child. But later, Althea's siblings, Millie, Ann, Lillian, and David, were born in New York.

During their first years in the city, Althea and her parents lived with her aunt, but the family eventually moved to an apartment on 143rd Street in Harlem. Remember the name of this street; it will play an important part in Althea's journey.

Though she loved her parents, and they loved her, Althea's home life was not ideal. Her parents found it difficult to manage her wild spirit. She didn't want to follow their rules or, really, anyone's rules. She spent much of her time in the neighborhood on her own, fighting with local kids or looking for adventure with her friends. Her desire for independence caused many arguments with her parents. She would often spend nights away from home with friends, much to the disappointment and worry of her parents.

Althea also didn't love school. She regularly skipped her classes to spend her days doing what she wanted to do. This often meant going to the movies, hanging out with friends, or playing ball. She was a tough, streetwise kid who knew how to take care of herself. But her parents were understandably upset on those days and nights when they couldn't find her.

One thing Althea did love was sports. She was tall, broadly built, fast, and enjoyed playing games that showcased her competitiveness and natural abilities. She especially liked sports like basketball and football but excelled at everything she played.

Luckily for Althea, finding games to play was as easy as walking out her front door. As part of a New York Police Athletic League program, 143rd Street was closed to traffic during the day and used as a playground for the local kids. It was on this street where Althea first learned to play paddle tennis. A cross between tennis and squash, paddle tennis would introduce her to a whole new world.

This is also the street where she met Buddy Walker. Buddy, a local entertainer and saxophone player, worked as a play leader at the playground. He spotted Althea playing paddle tennis and knew she had something special—special enough, even, to play tennis. Buddy was the first of many supporters Althea would meet who directly changed the course of her life. He took her under his wing, bought Althea her first tennis racquet, and began to train her in the sport of tennis.

Althea was intrigued by this new sport, and like every other sport, she gave it her best. She had a strong sense of confidence, even though she was young. And she didn't like to lose. After all, she had become the city-wide paddle tennis champion at the age of twelve, so why wouldn't she succeed at tennis too? She turned her paddle board skills into tennis skills and figured she could play with the best of them if given a chance.

As a well-known personality in the neighborhood, Buddy had a lot of connections. And he used those connections to get Althea into the Cosmopolitan Tennis Club, a private club for Black tennis players. At the club, Althea met Dr. Hubert Eaton and Dr. Robert W. Johnson. These two men were undoubtedly the most influential in Althea's life. The doctors, impressed by her ability on the court and her potential, offered to become her mentors. They gave her training and the opportunity to grow skills that she wouldn't have had otherwise.

The doctors entered her into her first ATA (American Tennis Association) tournament. The ATA was an organization created for

Black tennis players. It existed because the USTA (US Lawn Tennis Association) didn't allow Black people to compete in their tournaments or play on their courts. So, while entry into the ATA was a big step, it was as far as Althea could go. But little did the world know then that Althea would be the one to bring the USTA barriers crashing down.

In 1942, she debuted with a bang at the ATA New York State Girls' Championship at the age of fourteen. She easily won her matches, and Althea was overjoyed by her first tennis championship. It proved to others what she already knew—she was better than good; she had the potential to be great. She won the Girls' Championship again in 1944 and 1945. In 1947, Althea, now an adult, won her first ATA National Women's Singles Championship title. It was the first in a string of ten consecutive women's singles wins, solidifying her place as the best female Black tennis player of the time.

PATH TO SUCCESS

Drs. Eaton and Johnson knew Althea could go further with tennis. And soon, they made her an offer she couldn't refuse. They urged her to move to the South, where they could guide her tennis career. With their support, she packed her things and moved to Wilmington, Virginia, to Dr. Eaton's home. They also encouraged Althea to finish high school. Althea, who had dropped out of high school in New York, wasn't keen. But they insisted that a high school education was a necessary foundation for her future plans.

Althea was hesitant to take on such a big move. Everything and everyone she knew was in New York. But she also knew there was great opportunity for her if she followed this path. Friends encouraged her to try it out, and she followed their advice.

When she arrived at Dr. Eaton's home, Althea felt out of place. The Eatons were well off. They had nice things. Everything was clean and fresh—so different from what she was used to while living in New York. Althea couldn't believe her eyes or her luck. But everyone was welcoming, and soon Althea felt like she belonged.

Dr. Eaton, a prominent leader in the county, maintained a clay tennis court in the back of his home. Due to segregation, Black people weren't allowed on public courts in Wilmington. So, Dr. Eaton's home, with the only tennis court in the area, was always a hub of activity. This meant Althea always had partners to compete against and improve her skills.

Though her home base during summers was with Dr. Johnson in Lynchburg, Tennessee, they spent much of the time on the road. They traveled throughout the country to various tournaments where she could play against other top players in the ATA. Althea enjoyed the summers with Dr. Johnson, practicing at his home court and touring the ATA circuit with other fellow players under Dr. Johnson's tutelage. Althea got to visit new cities like Washington, Philadelphia, and other places.

Althea continued to play other sports during her high school years in Wilmington. She was on the school baseball team and was even elected basketball team captain. Althea had other talents, too. Musically inclined from a young age, she loved singing and playing the saxophone, an instrument she learned to play back in New York.

Althea spent three years with Dr. Eaton and her summers on the circuit route with Dr. Johnson. All these experiences helped her transform into an elite player. She also graduated high school at the end of her time in Wilmington. She went on to attend Florida A&M University on a full sports scholarship. Althea started her time in the South as a scared, unsure high school dropout and ended up a confident, self-assured undergraduate.

With her track record on the court at an all-time high, Althea continued to set herself apart from other players. She was considered the best Black female player in the country. And that distinction helped set the foundation for the significant changes that would come next.

Drs. Eaton and Johnson, while happy for Althea's progress in the ATA, had bigger plans for her. They wanted her to compete in the USTA Outdoor Nationals. This would be a momentous accomplishment if they could pull it off. No African American had ever done it before.

The doctors, various press outlets, the Black media, and other notable personalities pressed the USTA to accept Athea's application to play at one of the games. Under so much pressure, the USTA relented, relaxing their rule to receive her application to play in the Forest Hills tournament in New York in 1950. This was a historic event. With the eyes of the press and the tennis community on Althea, she became the first Black person to play at a USTA National game. While Althea didn't win the tournament, she played with such power and ability that no one could deny she was a serious contender in the sport.

Althea was thankful for all the people who believed in her and fought for her to have the opportunity to play in this historic match. And despite her loss, she was confident that she could play on a national stage and on the same level as any white opponent. Her star was on the rise, and the country was watching.

From there, Althea was invited to play in another tournament in Miami, where she became the first Black person to play a mixed tournament. The smaller USTA matches were stepping stones on the road to the greatest opportunity yet—the chance to play at Wimbledon.

With pressure on the USTA still strong and sixteen tournament wins under her belt, Althea was invited to play at Wimbledon in 1950. She would be the first African American to play on England's oldest and most famous court. Althea made it as far as the quarter finals, but she lost against Beverly Seed, 6-1, 6-3. Althea was devastated. She had come so far and done so well along the way to the biggest competition of her life. Despite the outcome, she had tried her hardest, and her outstanding performance made headlines and sparked debate on the inclusion of African Americans in sports. Althea was not yet at her peak, and before she would get there, circumstances would set her back a few years before becoming a legend.

TRIALS AND TRIBULATIONS

After her loss at Wimbledon in 1950, Althea tried again in 1951, '52, and '53 with no luck. Imagine working so hard and breaking so many boundaries to get to these competitions only to keep losing again and again. It was devastating for Althea and made her question her place in the tennis world.

Despite her presence on the court and inclusion by some in the tennis community, Althea was constantly scrutinized because she was Black. Her skin color made her the topic of conversation wherever she played and drew both good and bad attention. She felt like an object of curiosity by the press and the tennis community. It made her lonely and left her feeling like she could never really be herself or relax because no one else looked like her.

Althea, of course, wasn't new to this. After all, she went to school in the South and experienced segregation firsthand. There were rules that forbade Black people from interacting with or sharing the same space as whites. She was used to sitting at the back of the bus or movie theater and being denied access to places like tennis courts, hotels, and diners meant for whites only. But the familiarity of it didn't make experiencing it any easier. Segregation made no sense to her, and she was disheartened by it. "It disgusted me and made me feel ashamed in a way I'd never been ashamed back in New York,"[6] she said of her experiences with segregation in the South. Similarly, being the only Black person in the white-dominated world of tennis made her feel sad. It was a lonely path.

As her winning streak plummeted in the early 1950s, so did her love for the game. And even though she completed tournaments, she couldn't make a living off tennis. At the time, amateur players didn't receive prize money like professional players do today. Back then, the major tournaments, like the Grand Slams, only allowed amateur players to compete, and no prize money was given out. For this reason, tennis was predominantly a game for the rich or the elite, who could afford to play without pay. Things changed in 1968, when the Grand Slam tournaments opened up to both professional and amateur players, ushering in the modern era of tennis known as the Open Era.

Because she couldn't support herself through tennis, Althea had to find another way to make a living. After she graduated from Florida A&M, she became a physical education teacher at Lincoln University. She taught at the school for two years, from 1954 to 1955. And during that time, she considered leaving the game altogether.

Althea felt discouraged because she couldn't make her own way in tennis. Throughout her career, she always had sponsors, mentors, trainers, and supporters who helped her pursue her dreams. But she wanted to feel the independence that came with doing it on her own. After so many years and so many losses, Althea felt no

---

6 Gibson, Fitzgerald, and Joseph, *I Always Wanted to Be Somebody*.

passion for the game and thought she would be better off if she joined the Women's Army Corps, where she could make money and support herself.

But her then trainer, Sydney Llewellyn, urged her to send in an entry form for the upcoming USTA Nationals. And thankfully, she did. While she was at the Nationals, a USTA official approached her, offering her another opportunity that would take her down a different path. She and a few other high-profile tennis players were picked to go on a State Department goodwill tour of Asia in 1955.

That tour was her first introduction to the world outside the US and turned out to be just the pivot she needed to reignite her passion for the sport of tennis. As she toured from country to country playing exhibition games, Althea met new people, experienced different cultures, and rekindled her love for the game.

Fresh off the heels of the tour in 1956 and with renewed enthusiasm, Althea competed at Wimbledon. Her rankings had slipped, the odds weren't in her favor, and the mainstream press had no faith in her. She didn't win that year. But she would be back.

ACHIEVEMENTS

Following her Wimbledon loss in 1956, she entered the French Open in Paris, easily defeating her longtime nemesis, Angela Mortimer. Her win at the French Open made her the first Black player to win any major championship. It was her first Grand Slam, and it solidified her place as a top player in the world.

She was on fire in the two years that followed her French Open win. She returned to Wimbledon, eager for a second chance to take the title. Day after day as the tournament progressed and Althea won every match leading her closer to the finals, her confidence rose. By the time the finals between her and Darlene Hard were underway, Althea had no doubt the championship would be hers. In the heat of the London summer, Althea played a hard, fast game and defeated Darlene 6-3, 6-2. Her moment had finally arrived, and she soaked it all in.

During the medal ceremony, the Queen of England congratulated Althea and presented her with her trophy. And that's when Althea knew she had come a long way from New York. The wild child from Harlem had made a name for herself, and for as long as Althea could remember, that's all she had ever wanted. Later, Althea would say of her historic win, "This is the hour I will remember always as the crowning conclusion to a long and wonderful journey."[7]

Althea also won the singles title at the US Open that year. The following year, in 1958, she defended her Wimbledon and US Open titles, reclaiming her place as the No. 1 US tennis player. While she seemed unstoppable in the singles tournaments, she was also a powerhouse in the doubles tournaments, winning doubles titles in Wimbledon in 1957 and 1958 and the US and Australian doubles in 1957. In total, Althea won eleven Grand Slam titles.

In addition to these on-court firsts, Althea was also the first Black person to appear on the cover of *Sports Illustrated* in September 1957 and again in *Time Magazine* in August 1957. And probably the biggest honor of all, Althea was awarded Athlete of the Year in 1957 by the *Associated Press*, the first African American to do so. In 1971, Althea was inducted into the International Tennis Hall of Fame.

Even after she died in 2003, Althea was still breaking records. She was the first female athlete to receive a US Postal Service commemorative stamp in the Black Heritage Stamp series in 2013.

---

7 Gibson, Fitzgerald, and Joseph, *I Always Wanted to Be Somebody.*

LIFE LESSONS

Following her Grand Slam wins in 1957 and 1958, Althea was ranked the No. 1 player in the world. But even when you're the best, you sometimes are forced to make difficult decisions that will affect everything you've worked for. It's hard to believe, but at just thirty years old and the height of her career, Gibson had to step away from tennis in 1958. It was a huge blow to the tennis star, but she could not support her career or herself. Amateur tennis didn't pay, and she lacked the financial means of other tennis players to continue.

But Althea had packed so many achievements in the almost two decades she played; it seemed like she had played for a lifetime. Despite the discrimination she faced, she became one of the best tennis players in the world. Robert Ryland, a coach and tennis pioneer in his own right, once said of Althea, "She is one of the greatest players who ever lived. I think she'd beat the Williams sisters."[8] There's a statement that speaks volumes about Althea's skill and athleticism.

Though no title would ever be as great as those she carried in her tennis career, Althea stayed close to sports for the remainder of her life. First, she played with the world-famous basketball team, the Harlem Globetrotters. Then, at thirty-seven, she set her sights on golf, becoming the first Black woman to join the LPGA tour. And in 1976, Althea Gibson took a position as the first female athletic commissioner of New Jersey.

Althea's story can teach us a lot about life. Perhaps the greatest lesson is, we are not defined by our surroundings or circum-

---

8 Marea Donnelly, "Althea Gibson Broke Wimbledon Colour Barrier with First Singles Win," *The Daily Telegraph*, July 5, 2017, https://www.dailytelegraph.com .au/news/althea-gibson-broke-wimbledon-colour-barrier-with-first-singles-win /news-story/cc7f8c70848e2fa2bbe7fe7587cedb37.

stances. Though Althea had a rough upbringing and often found herself in trouble, she always believed she was destined for more. When opportunities were presented to her, she took them and worked hard to make the most of them.

A good support system can also be vital, especially when circumstances are stacked against you. Althea benefitted from the support of mentors, coaches, friends, fans, and other tennis players. They helped her through tough times and kept her believing in her abilities. But it's not just about who you know or luck; it's also about believing in yourself. Althea believed in herself and knew she was meant to achieve something great in life, and people and events aligned to help her on that road to greatness.

Althea broke down many color barriers and did so on her own terms. Though she was reluctant to be an outspoken activist, she contributed to bridging the racial divide in sports. With every win, she effectively brought change. Though she was the subject of debate and scrutiny, she didn't let it get in the way of her bigger dreams. She was literally the face that changed tennis, and her desire to succeed outweighed the racial disparity with which she was confronted.

"For me, she was the most important pioneer for tennis. She was Black, she looked like me, and she opened up so many doors,"[9] Serena Williams said of Althea Gibson, her idol. And because Althea broke down so many doors in the 1950s, many more were opened to the long line of Black tennis players who came after her. Thanks to Althea, players like the Williams sisters, Coco Gauff, Frances Tiafoe, and Sloane Stephens are household names.

---

9 "'The Most Important Pioneer for Tennis'—Althea Gibson's Great Legacy," Women's Tennis Association, August 25, 2020, https://www.wtatennis.com /news/1739180/the-most-important-pioneer-for-tennis-althea-gibson-s-great -legacy.

CHAPTER 2

BASEBALL

AARON JUDGE AND JACKIE ROBINSON

AARON JUDGE

"I play this game for the fans. I've got a passion for this, and I've got a gift. I do it for them. I do it for the kids, rocking my jersey in the stands and one day wishing they're out there at Yankee Stadium. That's what it's all about: trying to inspire kids to do something special with their life, whichever avenue they go."[10]

EARLY YEARS

What's it like to hit a home run? Or better yet, the most home runs in the American League (AL)? To find out, we only need to turn to Aaron Judge, the New York Yankees right fielder, for that answer. In 2022, Aaron broke a long-standing AL record, becoming the player with the most home runs in a season. Whether setting records or breaking them, this young slugger has been one to watch since his early college days. And it's his positive attitude, team mentality, and intense focus that's made him one of the best players in baseball.

For Aaron, it all started on April 26, 1992, the day he was born. From the beginning, his story was unique. Aaron James Judd was born in a Sacramento hospital and adopted the very next day. Teachers Patty and Wayne Judge brought him home to join their small family. Aaron would be the second child for the Judges, who had another son, John, waiting back home for the arrival of his new

---

10 Tom Verducci, "Aaron Judge: The Authentic Home Run King," *Sports Illustrated*, October 5, 2022, https://www.si.com/mlb/2022/10/05/aaron-judge-authentic -home-run-king.

brother. John was also an adopted child. With their family complete, the Judges set about raising their children in the farm town of Linden, California, a quiet place with an appealing small-town culture and friendly neighborhoods.

Aaron grew up in a loving home and among a tight-knit community. He played ball with his neighborhood friends and flourished under his parents' care. They instilled in him values that upheld the importance of family, community, giving back, and education, and he leaned on that foundation many times in his life.

But by the age of eleven, Aaron, who is biracial, wondered why he didn't look like his parents, who were white. The Judges sat down with him and explained to him that he was adopted. For many children, learning they are adopted can be difficult to hear and harder yet to understand. But the news of his adoption didn't faze young Aaron. Instead, he accepted the explanation with little fuss, happy to know the truth. Of the revelation, Aaron said, "Nothing really changed. I honestly can't even remember too much because it wasn't that big of a deal. They just told me I was adopted, and I said, 'Okay, can I go outside and play?'"[11]

Growing up, Aaron was a tall kid, and his height and large stature drew a lot of attention. As the years went by, he continued to outgrow his peers. Today, Aaron is one of the largest players on the field, weighing around 282 pounds and standing six feet, seven inches tall. He's taller than most players in Major League Baseball (MLB) and the largest position player in the MLB. Because of his build, many thought he would play sports like basketball and football. And growing up, he loved all three of them equally, but baseball would eventually win his heart.

---

[11] Lucas Casaletto, "Aaron Judge: 'I Wouldn't Be a New York Yankee If It Wasn't for My Mom,'" The Score, December 8, 2023, https://www.thescore.com/mlb/news/1300236.

Aaron was an all-around athlete, meaning he was good at many sports. Throughout high school, he played on the basketball, football, and baseball teams. But he wasn't just a good ballplayer; he was also an excellent student.

Though he played on many teams, his parents made sure he kept up with his studies. Education always came first. Aaron maintained good grades throughout his academic career.

Top universities and colleges scouted Aaron during his senior year, all wanting him to play for their sports teams. But he was torn. He didn't know which sport he should pursue. He even received an early offer to play professionally from the Oakland A's, who selected him in a 2010 draft pick when he was eighteen. But school was important to him and his parents; he didn't want to skip out on a college education. So, Aaron turned down the offer.

As Aaron grappled with his decision, he realized he loved baseball just a little more than the other sports. The realization helped shift his focus from *what* to do to *where* to go. He decided on California State University in Fresno, where he received a full scholarship and could still be close to his family.

While in university, he played for the Fresno State Bulldogs, and from the very beginning, Aaron made an impression. He was a powerful player with a winning swing. His coach, Mike Batesole, thought he was special. He believed Aaron was even good enough to play the demanding outfielder position. Players in this position need speed, agility, good instincts, and a strong throwing arm, all of which Aaron possessed. He played both right and center field.

Aaron was a star baseball player at Fresno State. After his three years with the Bulldogs, he had a .345 batting average and eighteen home runs to show for his time. But what is a batting average, and why does it matter? A player's batting average is one of the most relevant stats in baseball. It is calculated by dividing the number of times a player hits the ball by the number of times they go to bat. The average player bats around .250, and a good player around .300. Aaron was already batting way above average.

In 2011 and 2012, Aaron helped take his team to the College World Series. But it was his performance at the 2012 College Home Run Derby where he made a mark. He made one thrilling home run after another, surpassing the competition. He won the derby with a final tally of sixteen home runs. The College Derby singled him out as a player to watch. Scouts from the major leagues were paying close attention.

Something big was just on the horizon.

PATH TO SUCCESS

With one more year of university, the New York Yankees selected Aaron as their first-round draft pick. This was a big deal. The world-famous Yankees, known for winning twenty-seven World Series titles, the most by far of any professional baseball team, wanted Aaron. He had always dreamed of playing professionally, and here was his chance. He accepted and was excited to begin this new chapter.

While it seemed like Aaron had it made, he still had a lot to prove. And that started with his time in the minor leagues. The minor leagues are an essential step in major league baseball. Like all rookies, Aaron had to make his way through the lower levels of the minors before he could play in the majors. Not an easy feat considering there are five levels of the minor leagues: Rookie, Single-A, High-A, Double-A, and Triple-A. Major league teams pull only the best players from Triple-A teams to play in their games. It's normal for players to spend a season at each level of the minor leagues, which could mean anywhere from four to five years. The minors help players improve their game and prepare them for the demands of major league baseball.

Aaron had to make his way up this ladder before even considering playing in a major league game. He had to put in a lot of practice, time, and hard work. But Aaron was determined to do his best. He initially debuted with the Scottsdale Scorpions in 2013. But just after the draft pick, Aaron tore a muscle in his leg. He couldn't play for the rest of the season. It was a bad turn of events for a rookie learning the ropes.

But Aaron returned in 2014 to play with the Charleston River Dogs, where he impressed everyone who watched. He quickly moved up the levels of the minor leagues, going from rookie to Triple-A in roughly three years. After the River Dogs in 2014, he played for the Tampa Tarpons and Trenton Thunder in 2015. In 2016, he joined a Triple-A team, the Scranton/Wilkes-Barre RailRiders.

Though his averages were solid, Aaron struggled to find his groove, but the Yankees had high hopes for him and what he could bring to the team.

So when he started spring training in 2015, the Yankees invited him to the major league camp to train. This move solidified their investment in Aaron and ignited his desire to play in the major leagues. Aaron was honored to train with some of baseball's best players and his idols. It was an unforgettable opportunity that intensified his desire to make it to the majors. He hoped to be back as a permanent member soon.

Each level of the minors got more challenging as Aaron made his way to Triple-A, and maintaining consistently high averages took some work. He even went through a slump where his averages reached an all-time low. His batting average was just .221. But

Aaron rallied. Taking advice from those around him and working hard daily, he bounced back. His turnaround impressed the Yankees managers and coaches. And that turning point paid off.

The Yankees, who had been on a losing streak, were making changes to the team. They needed fresh players who could bring some energy and, hopefully, some wins. And Aaron was a top prospect. What happened next was a dream come true for Aaron and a validation of all his hard work.

On August 12, 2016, in the middle of his Triple-A season with Scranton/Wilkes-Barre, Aaron got an unexpected call to play for the Yankees. He was at a local Rochester, New York, restaurant enjoying a late-night dinner with his parents. His team had just played the Rochester Red Wings and won, and during the game, he delivered his nineteenth home run for the season. He was tired but exhilarated.

The team's manager, Al Pedrique, came into the restaurant and approached Aaron and his family with the good news. Aaron would later say, "I was shocked. I was still waiting for my food. I was hungry. It really didn't hit me. My parents start going crazy. My mom's crying, everyone's happy."[12]

But there was a catch. The Yankees wanted him to play a game the next day. Sure, it was last-minute, but it was also the opportunity of a lifetime. Aaron had no intention of letting it pass him by. With no time to waste, he and his parents made the long overnight drive to New York City. Excited, enthusiastic, and eager, Aaron arrived at Yankee Stadium without sleep the following day.

---

12 Eddie Matz, "Hop in the Back, Mom and Dad Are Driving! What It's Really Like Getting Called Up to the Majors," ESPN, August 30, 2019, https://www.espn.com /mlb/story/_/id/27468317/hop-back-mom-dad-driving-really-getting-called -majors.

On August 13, 2016, Aaron made his professional debut in the MLB against the Tampa Bay Rays. With his quick climb up the minors and his track record thus far, the pressure was on him to deliver. He was eighth at bat, and he had a hard act to follow. Tyler Austin, who also made his MLB debut with the Yankees that day, hit a home run just before Aaron came to bat. Would Aaron be so lucky?

The pitches from Matt Andriese, the Tampa Bay pitcher, came at him quickly. After the first two pitches, Aaron was down 2-0 after failing to connect. But with the crack of his bat on the third try, he hit a monstrous home run down center field into the netting. The ball traveled 446 feet. What a debut! He and Austin became the first teammates to hit back-to-back home runs in their MLB debuts. With his history-making swing, there was a promising start for Aaron in the majors. Aaron made a second home run that day, which contributed to the Yankees winning the game 8-4 against Tampa Bay.

But it wasn't all smooth sailing for Aaron.

TRIALS AND TRIBULATIONS

Despite his running start, things fell apart early in Aaron's first year with the Yankees. He had a lot of strikeouts and few hits. His batting average had slipped to .179, and by mid-season, he'd only hit four home runs. Things had gone downhill quickly, and his low batting average constantly reminded him how far he had fallen. And to make things worse, Aaron strained his oblique muscle that year. The injury benched him for the rest of the season, and he wouldn't play again until 2017.

During that year, Aaron struggled through some difficult times. He fell into a mid-season slump that would last months, where he made a habit of missing pitches and striking out. But Aaron never felt defeated. He knew this was just another part of baseball. He maintained a clear head and a positive outlook. "For me, it's just that time of year. Everyone goes through these ups and downs. You are going to get out of this. It's just part of baseball. . . . I just have to keep grinding; it will all work out,"[13] Aaron said of his challenges that year. He stuck with it and stayed positive, and in return his 2017 season turned out to be one of his best.

Injuries continued to plague Aaron as the years progressed. A broken wrist caused by a pitch from a fastball kept him out of the game for two months during the 2018 season. And in 2019, he was back on the injured list with another oblique strain. In 2020, a fractured rib caused his lung to collapse, and a calf injury kept Aaron off the field for some time. However, because of the COVID-19 pandemic, the 2020 season had a late start, which gave Aaron enough time to recuperate from his fractured rib and salvage the year.

In baseball, like most sports, injuries are common. Aaron tackled frequent injuries by adapting training methods to improve his conditioning. He incorporated stretching, mobility, and core exercises to help his body stay flexible and strong.

When the 2021 season started, Aaron faced a different type of challenge. His contract with the Yankees was up at the end of the season. He loved being a Yankee, and it saddened him he couldn't reach a deal with management on his contract. Aaron knew his worth and wasn't happy with the deal they offered him. But he didn't want to play the season with the contract negotiation

13 Kevin Kernan, "Aaron Judge's Star Power Is Slump-Proof for Now," *New York Post*, August 14, 2017, https://nypost.com/2017/08/14/aaron-judge-takes -another-giant-leap-toward-superstardom.

unsettled, so he ended the talks until the season was over. He decided to become a free agent if a deal still couldn't be reached.

When the season ended, there was no movement on the deal. Other teams contacted Aaron, hoping to entice him to leave New York. But all he wanted was to stay with the Yankees. It was a difficult time for Aaron, not knowing where he would end up. But in the end, the Yankees knew they couldn't let him go. They offered him one of the biggest deals in MLB—a deal that would make him a Yankee for life.

ACHIEVEMENTS

Aaron has been breaking records since his first home run as an MLB rookie. And though his story has had a few rough patches, it's been an incredible ride to the top.

After his rough start in 2016, Aaron knew he had to do better the following season. It would be his first full year as a Yankee, and he had something to prove. Home run after home run, he wowed the crowds and impressed managers and teammates alike. Aaron's achievements in 2017 permanently placed his name in baseball history.

He set the record for the most home runs by a rookie in a season. Aaron hit fifty-two home runs, surpassing Joe DiMaggio's record of twenty-nine set in 1936. All eyes were now on Aaron. His strong performance during the year earned him four American League Rookie of the Month titles, and then, the prized American League Rookie of the Year award.

During the 2017 mid-season break, Aaron won the All-Star Home Run Derby, beating out top players. He was the first rookie ever to do so. If Aaron wasn't a sensation before, winning the All-Star Derby made him the talk of the baseball world.

Early on, Aaron attracted crowds, and the Yankees knew they had a star on their hands. At that point, Yankee management did something no MLB team had ever done. They created a special section in the stands at Yankee Stadium for Aaron's biggest fans and named it after him. In the "Judge's Chamber," fans dressed like traditional court judges with black robes and white wigs; they waved Styrofoam gavels and chanted Aaron's name. The "Judge's Chamber" birthed a new slogan and nickname, "All Rise"—a nickname Aaron has embraced.

If Aaron's 2017 year sounds exciting, 2022 was even better when he hit sixty-two home runs in one season. It was his biggest record-breaking stat yet and a new AL record! Yankee great Roger Maris was the last to hold the record of sixty-one home runs back in 1961.

That year, the pressure increased as Aaron came closer and closer to Maris's record. But he took it all in stride, remaining humble and focused. When Aaron reached fifty-eight home runs, the Yankees began using specially marked balls for authentication. Everyone knew they were watching history in the making. The fandom was at a fever pitch as onlookers anticipated a home run at every game. And Aaron rarely disappointed. He kept hitting home runs, to everyone's amazement. At fifty-eight home runs, Aaron was among a small group of American League legends to do so. Only four players in one hundred years had hit fifty-eight home runs. And once he reached sixty-two home runs in October, in a game against the Texas Rangers, Aaron was now in a league of his own.

After the historic signing of his contract in 2022, Aaron was named captain of the New York Yankees, an incredible honor signifying how much the team and management believed in Aaron. Among the awards he won that year, he received The Associated Press

Male Athlete of the Year and the American League Most Valuable Player awards.

In 2023, Aaron received the Roberto Clemente Award, baseball's highest honor. It was given to Aaron for his work with his charitable organization, "All Rise," which helps kids reach their potential.

In other achievements, Aaron was named to the All-Star MLB game five times in 2017, 2018, 2020, 2021, and 2022. Only the best of the best are chosen to play in the All-Stars. He has also been a three-time recipient of the Silver Slugger Award in 2017, 2021, and 2022.

LIFE LESSONS

Small-town boy turned major league captain makes for an amazing headline. But what got Aaron to the top was more than just his athletic ability or drive for success. It was his value system, his teamwork, and his humility. Aaron never let his meteoric rise to the top get to his head. Instead, he always placed focus on the team and the achievements of every player on the team. For Aaron, it was never a one-person show. Everything he does is for the good of the club.

From fans to teammates to managers, everyone admires Aaron. Joe Girardi, former Yankees manager, praised Aaron, saying, "He's never lost who he is and his ability to change someone's day. He's a natural-born leader for me. . . . It's almost like he's a big brother. He watches out over everyone."[14] There's undoubtedly a long line of people who feel the same about Aaron.

---

14 "Aaron Judge of New York Yankees Ties Mark McGwire for Home Runs by Rookie," ESPN, September 25, 2017, https://www.espn.com/mlb/story/_/id/20816622/aaron-judge-new-york-yankees-ties-mark-mcgwire-home-runs-rookie.

But what does Aaron himself think of his accomplishment? "Anytime individual records, individual awards are given, it's never individual. It's never single-handedly done. It's through a group effort. People behind the scenes, family support, friends, teammates. So, I can't stand up here and say this is a great accomplishment for me. This is something for my family, for my teammates, for the Yankees. This is a group effort that I'm happy to share,"[15] Aaron said. By both acknowledging those who supported him and dedicating the record to the team, Aaron showed why he is a beloved leader.

With his achievements, Aaron has earned a place in baseball history and undoubtedly left a legacy that will stand the test of time. And he may still break some of his own records. Only time will tell. As Aaron himself said, "So what everybody expects out of me, that's nothing compared to what I'm trying to do every single day. So it's constant motivation."[16] The AL "Home Run King," known as much for his masterful swing as his personality, has shown us that greatness and humility can coexist.

15 "Judge on Breaking AL Home Run Record," MLB, October 5, 2022, https://www.mlb.com/video/judge-on-breaking-al-home-run-record.

16 FOX Sports, "J. P. Morosi Sits Down with Yankees Star, Aaron Judge | FOX MLB," YouTube, August 3, 2019, https://www.youtube.com /watch?v=sSOb2uq5IqA.

JACKIE ROBINSON

....
"A life is not important except in the
impact it has on other lives."[17]
....

EARLY YEARS

What would you do if you were chosen to do something extraordinary? Something that had never been done before? Do you think you'd be excited, nervous, scared? Jackie Robinson was asked to do something that would change a nation. And as the first Black player to play major league baseball, he experienced all those emotions and more.

On January 31, 1919, Jackie Robinson was the youngest child born to sharecroppers Mallie and Jerry Robinson. The names of his older brothers were Edgar, Frank, and Mack, and his sister was Willa Mae. The family lived together in Cairo, Georgia, for a time. But when Jackie was six months old, his father unexpectedly left the family. Faced with the difficult job of raising the children alone, Jackie's mother decided moving closer to family in California would be best. Jackie's family headed west to Pasadena when he was just sixteen months old.

In Pasadena, life wasn't much easier. Jackie's mother worked hard but still found it difficult to support the family on her own. She

---

17 Jackie Robinson, *I Never Had It Made: An Autobiography of Jackie Robinson*, (NY: HarperCollins, 1995).

often relied on government assistance to get by. Food and other essentials were scarce. But the one thing that was abundant in the Robinson household was love. Millie Robinson always had time for her children and instilled in them a love for family. She raised them to value religion, be compassionate to others, and respect themselves. Above all, she wanted them to have more than she ever had, so a solid education was also important to her.

Jackie Robinson grew up during segregation when the separation of whites and Blacks was legal in America. The Civil Rights Act of 1964 was still years in the future, so Jackie and the rest of his African American friends and peers weren't allowed to do the same things white children did. Black children couldn't attend the same schools, play on the same playgrounds, or use the same recreational areas. Black people were barred from many restaurants, hotels, stores, and more. And if they were allowed into a whites-only space, there were firm restrictions, like race-specific train cars and water fountains. Jackie became aware of the divide when he was eight years old, and it made him resentful.

Within this environment, racism and prejudice were regular occurrences in Jackie's young life. Whether it was other children, neighbors, or strangers, Jackie learned that being Black often meant being on the other end of someone's hatred and fear, and he had a hard time making sense of it. But his mother taught him no matter how much hatred or mistreatment he came across, he had the same rights as anyone else. From her, he also learned how to be patient and keep cool in tense situations, which would serve him well in a segregated society and his baseball career.

Jackie was a streetwise kid who spent much of his time with his friends in the neighborhood. He showed a natural talent for sports early on. At John Muir Technical High, he was on the football, baseball, basketball, and track teams. He was excellent at all four sports, gaining the attention of colleges and universities that offered him athletic scholarships. But Jackie, who loved and respected his mother dearly, wanted to stay close to home. So, he chose the University of California, Los Angeles (UCLA).

At UCLA, he did his best to excel. He continued to play the same four sports he'd played in high school and earned varsity letters for each, becoming the first person ever to do so. While Jackie enjoyed his initial years at college, his time at UCLA wasn't without struggles and challenges. After two years, Jackie decided to leave university. He felt discouraged. College life wasn't real life. No matter how hard he tried or what he achieved in college, academically or athletically, his options were limited. He was dismayed by the lack of opportunities for Black people—even those with a higher education. He felt there was no real future in sports for an African American man like himself because Black athletes were kept out of professional sports. The invisible color barrier made it impossible for a Black athlete to make a living from sports. With this in mind, Jackie wondered what the point of being good at something was if he couldn't do anything with it.

Jackie also left school because, more than anything, he wanted to work to help support his mom, and he couldn't do that if there were no well-paying jobs for Black athletes. Jackie spent some time looking for a path that would help him support his mother and help kids, something he was passionate about. He eventually accepted an offer to be athletic director for the National Youth Administration. But before he could really begin his career, World War II broke out. Jackie was drafted into the Army in 1942, marking the beginning of a new chapter in his life.

Jackie did his basic training at Fort Riley in Kansas, and within a few months, he completed Officer Candidate School and became a second lieutenant in January 1943. But even in the Army, Jackie couldn't escape the inequalities of segregation. He faced many issues of racial injustice. He called it out whenever he witnessed unfair treatment, and he never backed down, even when faced with hostility or punishment. He always stood up for his rights and those of his fellow Black officers, taking concerns to the highest office. The men under his charge were thankful for Jackie's advocacy, which earned him their respect. His determination helped bring about some much-needed changes in the unit.

But Jackie's resistance wasn't appreciated by many. And in one incident, it almost cost him his future. One day, Jackie refused to move to the back of the bus, the designated area for Black people, while on a ride back to the base. The bus driver confronted Jackie and told him to move. But Jackie refused. The driver couldn't believe Jackie's defiance and got angrier and angrier. The confrontation escalated and ultimately led to a court-martial trial for Jackie. Thankfully, he was acquitted of all charges, and soon after, he received an honorable discharge from the Army in 1944. Jackie was happy to be out of the Army but wondered what he would do next.

Jackie had heard from a fellow officer that the all-Black professional baseball team, the Kansas City Monarchs, was looking for players. He tried out and was accepted. While definitely a step forward, he soon became weary of the harsh realities that faced Black baseball teams. Unlike their white counterparts, Black teams didn't have the same money, support, or promotion as the white teams, and the players suffered for it. Aside from chaotic travel schedules and little rest between games, there were rarely any places where African American players could stay or eat. Life on the road was hard. And Jackie grew to dislike it. He later said, "I began to wonder why I should dedicate my life to a career where the boundaries for progress were set by racial discrimination."[18] He had reached another point where being Black had boxed him in with no hope of advancement. But he was unsure of what he should or could do next.

Little did Jackie know things were about to change in a big way. His stay with the Monarchs was short-lived, lasting only five months before being recruited for the biggest job of his life.

PATH TO SUCCESS

In New York, the Brooklyn Dodgers General Manager and President, Branch Rickey, had heard about Jackie, and he wanted him for an extraordinary job. This job would bring national attention to the young player.

Rickey had an idea and was intent on doing something that had never been done before in professional baseball. He wanted to integrate his team with Black players. Rickey was passionate about justice and baseball. He knew the game would be better, more appealing, and more profitable if everyone, no matter their race, were allowed to play.

He also knew this "noble experiment," as it came to be known, would be difficult to carry out; there would be opposition, outrage, and even violence. Everything was at stake, and the risks were high. If the experiment worked, it would lead to the desegregation of professional baseball. If it failed, it would set progress back and jeopardize his career and that of the player he chose. Rickey wanted a player who was strong enough to maintain composure even in the most severe circumstances. After an exhaustive search lasting many months and spanning the US and other countries, he chose Jackie Robinson.

---

18 Robinson, *I Never Had It Made.*

Branch Rickey knew that Jackie had the ability of a star baseball player; his scouts had told him that. But what he needed from Jackie was something more. For this job, the right person would have to be courageous, level-headed, and strong-willed to face the opposition that would come their way. He invited Jackie to meet with him, hoping he had found the right man for the job.

When Jackie met Branch Rickey and heard about the plan, he had all the emotions you could imagine. He was happy, excited, nervous, and worried. This opportunity was life-changing in so many ways but also scary. Branch Rickey had bet on Jackie Robinson, and the future of integrated baseball depended on him being right.

In that meeting, Branch Rickey asked Jackie, "Have you got the guts to play the game no matter what happens?"[19] Rickey knew Jackie would face terrible hatred, anger, threats, and acts of violence by baseball fans and players alike, and he told him so. He even went as far as enacting the situations Jackie might face. He wanted to prepare Jackie for the worst. And beyond that, he wanted Jackie to understand the toll it would take on him, as he was expected to turn the other cheek to hurtful comments, racist slurs, and abuse. Jackie was stunned and overwhelmed. But he also grasped what Rickey asked of him. And it made him wonder if he was up for this challenge. He knew this plan was bigger than he was. Jackie already felt the heavy burden, but he knew it would mean everything for the future of Black athletes in baseball and other sports if he succeeded. He felt such a deep responsibility for the Black children who would look up to him, for his family, and for the cause. In the end, he agreed.

---

19 Robinson, *I Never Had It Made.*

But before he could join the major leagues with the Dodgers, he, like all other baseball players, had to begin in the minors and work his way up. On October 23, 1945, Jackie signed his contract with the Montreal Royals, the Dodgers minor league team. Until that day, Branch Rickey's plans were a secret. No one knew he wanted to desegregate the Dodgers, let alone baseball.

The press were invited to the announcement, and the news floored them. The press, eager to share the news of Branch Rickey's radical move, had much to say. Would a Black player really make it to the major leagues? Could Black and white athletes play together? What would be the reaction of the fans and the players? That day, Jackie got his first taste of the media spotlight, and it didn't feel good. While there were some positive reports, mainly from the Black press and supportive white columnists, many news stories were negative. They believed Jackie couldn't cut it, wasn't a good enough player, and didn't belong in the white major leagues. This bumpy relationship with the press would last throughout his early career. After the announcement became public, there was a firestorm of activity. Everyone, from team owners to players, had something to say, and it was mostly all negative. They didn't want to see a Black man in the majors, and they made it clear.

Jackie started with the Montreal Royals in 1946. Initially, he found it hard as a rookie. Many players weren't friendly or avoided him altogether. But thankfully, there was one player, Lou Rochelli, who welcomed Jackie, helped him, and made his early days as a Royal tolerable.

Jackie worked hard to prove he belonged on the team. He knew Rickey was counting on him to do well. But he needed some adjustment time. He had a strong, fast throwing arm, but his batting average had slipped. He had fallen into a slump, unable to deliver the big hits he needed. But Jackie put all his efforts into training hard.

In his first game on April 18, 1946, things took an exciting turn when the Royals faced their parent team, the Dodgers, in an exhibition game at City Island Ballpark. Jackie was exhilarated by the relatively peaceful reception he received from the crowd. He had been so worried about what would happen when he came out. And as he played, he found he gained more confidence. He even hit a three-run home run. He had a resurgence of energy. Within time, Jackie came out of his slump, and as his season with the Royals continued, he proved himself to be an asset to the team. His teammates warmed to him, realizing he was not only a good player but a pivotal one, too.

But even more impressive, Jackie's presence on the field attracted Black fans to the game. Even though they encountered hostile situations, African Americans came out in droves to see Jackie Robinson play.

At the end of his season with the Royals, he was the league's top batter and had a .349 batting average. His team won the pennant and the International League playoffs.

And with such an impressive season, Jackie got the call he had been waiting for. It was time to play for the Dodgers.

Many Dodgers players were upset to hear that a Black man would join their team. Some even signed a petition saying they would not play with him on the field. But Rickey told the players they could accept it or leave. Jackie Robinson was going to play with the Dodgers, and that was the end of it.

Jackie was given the #42 jersey and played his first game with the Dodgers on April 15, 1947, at Ebbets Field in Brooklyn, New York.

The stands were overflowing with people who turned out to see the first professional Black player. Despite this history-making day, it wasn't Jackie's best performance. He played below his expectations, and that soon led to another slump. It was to be expected. The pressure, the tension on the team, and the continued negative media attention took their toll on him. Jackie found solace in his supporters like the Black media, Rickey, the fans who were rooting for him, and another player on the team named Harold Henry "Peewee" Reese, who supported Jackie early on.

Before the season was over, Jackie pulled out of the slump and thereafter proved to be an integral part of the team. He played every game with vigor, racking up runs, covering bases, supporting his teammates, and contributing to the team in every way. Despite his large size, he was agile and quick, which made him good at running and stealing bases, something he became well-known for. He had a strong throwing arm as well as a powerful swing. And he didn't have an ego like some other players. He always put the team first.

He finished his first year with the Dodgers with unimaginable success, winning awards and praise from fans and critics. And over the next few years of his baseball career, the spotlight would continue to shine down on him.

TRIALS AND TRIBULATIONS

The year 1947 was remarkable for Jackie Robinson, but it came with a heavy cost. As the first Black player to break the color line in baseball, Jackie had to endure many injustices, threats, jeers, and taunts from fans and even from other players. He was booed at, had objects thrown at him, and had to suffer the indignities of segregation, often forbidden to eat or sleep where his teammates did. He wasn't a media favorite, and they often made things harder for him.

As the team traveled around the country playing games, Jackie was on the receiving end of some of the worst displays of racism. Those who opposed his inclusion in the game used many tactics, from locked ballparks to threats of arrest, to ensure Jackie wouldn't play.

From his early minor league days to his time in the majors, Jackie endured racial incidences in both his professional and personal life. And what he experienced affected him greatly. Jackie questioned himself, his path, and whether this experiment would work. He didn't know if he really had what it took to turn the other cheek every time he came face to face with hatred or aggression. He longed to stand up for himself or retaliate, as he was used to doing in the past. It wore on him, and sometimes, he felt like he was at a breaking point. But he knew he had to see it through. So many people's hopes and dreams were riding on him. And he was keenly aware of his place in history. He knew he had to make it work for the many Black children who looked up to him, his family, future Black athletes, Branch Rickey, and the fight for equality. He had to show everyone that Black people could play alongside whites and were just as skilled, talented, and capable.

While the adversity Jackie endured was challenging, it made the team stronger. They realized they would have to work together to become a winning team. And working together meant accepting Jackie and standing up for him when he was wronged.

In the end, Jackie never let what he was feeling or his experiences stop him. As Branch Rickey asked, he showed restraint even in the toughest situations. Along the way, he gained the respect of his teammates and the nation.

"I had started the season as a lonely man. . . . I ended it feeling like a member of a solid team. The Dodgers were a championship team because all of us had learned something. I had learned how to exercise self-control—to answer insults, violence and injustice with silence. They had learned that it's not skin color but talent and ability that counts."[20]

Jackie Robinson played for the Dodgers for ten years, but by his final year, he was exhausted by all he had been through. His love for the game had waned. He did what he had set out to do and much more. By all accounts, the experiment had been a success. Many other major league teams now included Black players. The color line was broken. And with that achievement complete, Jackie felt he could say goodbye to baseball with no regrets.

ACHIEVEMENTS

In his time with the Brooklyn Dodgers, the team made it to six league championships. And Jackie achieved many more accomplishments during his years with the team.

In 1947, he received the Rookie of the Year award from the *Baseball Writers' Association of America* and the *Sporting News*. The crowds responded enthusiastically as the exhibition games he played in 1948 brought out record numbers of fans, many of whom were Black. And the fans would continue to support Jackie throughout his career.

In 1947, he also received the MLB Rookie of the Year award. And for five years straight, from 1949–1954, Jackie Robinson was chosen to play in the All-Star games.

---

20 Robinson, *I Never Had It Made.*

In 1949, with a batting average of .349, Jackie earned the National League's Most Valuable Player title and the Silver Bat award.

A career high for Jackie came in October 1955 when he helped the Dodgers team win their first World Series. He played in six of the seven games and went to bat twenty-two times. He even stole home base in a risky play at a critical point in game one, which helped reenergize the team.

After ten years of playing, Robinson's baseball career was one for the history books. By his retirement in 1957, he had achieved "a .313 batting average, 972 runs scored, 1,563 hits, and 200 stolen bases."[21] It was a sensational career that made him one of the shining lights of baseball.

In 1962, Jackie was the first Black player inducted into the Baseball Hall of Fame. It was a fitting honor for the man who was the first Black pioneer in baseball history.

In 1984, Jackie was awarded the Presidential Medal of Freedom. The prestigious award, the highest in the US for a nonmilitary person, recognizes individuals who have made significant contributions globally or in the United States within various sectors.

Jackie's jersey, # 42, was retired by the MLB in 1997. No other player would ever be assigned that number. But once a year, on April 15, every player wears #42. On Jackie Robinson Day, all teams in the MLB wear his number in honor of the man, his contributions to the game of baseball, and the advancement of civil rights. Jackie's number is the only one to be retired across all major league teams.

---

21 "Robinson, Jackie | Baseball Hall of Fame," Baseball Hall of Fame, accessed March 17, 2024, https://baseballhall.org/hall-of-famers/robinson-jackie.

LIFE LESSONS

In Jackie Robinson's case, success was never just about the game. So much was riding on the success of his integration into baseball. And he knew it. He carried a heavy burden but did so with honor and grace.

As the first Black man to play in the major leagues, he had the hopes and fears of African Americans on his shoulders. It was a solitary path at times, but it was also one that inspired hundreds of thousands of people.

He made it possible for African Americans and players of other races to play America's game. His performance showed the nation that Black and white people could work together and that Black people were equal and should have the same rights as white Americans. Branch Rickey called him "a credit to baseball and to America,"[22] and he was right.

Jackie could never have envisioned the turn his life would take. How could he have known that the boy who dropped out of UCLA and later said, "I never expected the walls to come tumbling down in my lifetime"[23] would not only witness the dismantling of the color line but be the one to start it all?

Sometimes, we are chosen for great things—things we could never imagine. We may even feel like we're not the right person for the job. But even then, know if you are chosen, it is for a reason.

Many years after his first World Series game in 1947, Jackie recalled his journey and his far-reaching impact on so many lives. He said, "There I was, the Black grandson of a slave, the son of a Black

---

22 "9 Quotes about Jackie Robinson," JackieRobinson.org, accessed March 17, 2024, https://jackierobinson.org/news/9-quotes-about-jackie-robinson.
23 Robinson, *I Never Had It Made*.

sharecropper, part of a historic occasion, a symbolic hero of my people."[24]

Jackie Robinson proved that even when you doubt your purpose, you can persevere and achieve the unimaginable. He will be remembered not only as one of the best baseball players to ever play the game but also for changing the face of sports and the mind of a country.

---

24 Robinson, *I Never Had It Made.*

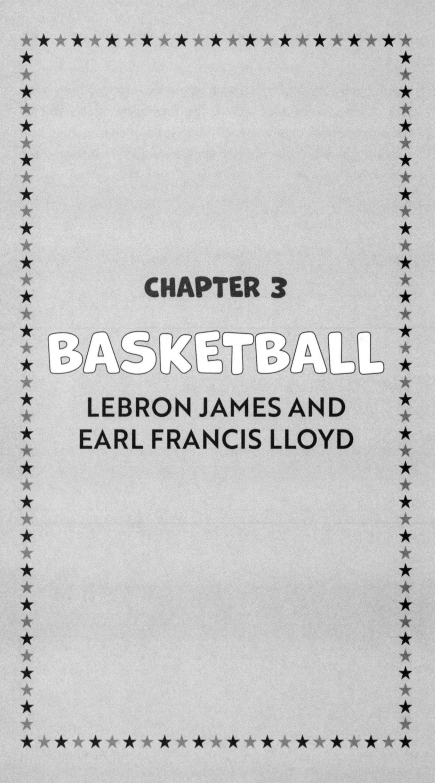

CHAPTER 3

BASKETBALL

LEBRON JAMES AND
EARL FRANCIS LLOYD

LEBRON JAMES

"Work hard with a plan. . . . You have got to be willing to do the work. Don't be afraid of hard work; embrace it because the harder you work, the closer you get to your goals. In those moments when you feel tired, when you feel like giving up, remember your plan. It's your anchor. It's what's going to keep you going when everything else tells you to quit. Your plan is your commitment, your promise to yourself that you won't stop until you have achieved what you set out to."[25]

EARLY YEARS

They call him "King James," and for good reason. LeBron James is one of the world's most iconic and celebrated basketball players. From his early start on an Amateur Athletic Union (AAU) basketball team to his epic rise in the NBA, he has reigned over the basketball court like no other. For his superstar performances, he has earned four NBA championship wins, countless awards, and the adoration of millions of fans.

Gloria James was just sixteen when she gave birth to her son, LeBron Raymone James, on December 30, 1984. LeBron's father, Anthony McClelland, also a teenager, was unable to handle the pressures of raising a child, and he abandoned Gloria and LeBron early on. Gloria was left to raise LeBron alone in Akron, Ohio, where he grew up.

---

25 Aim Arena, "Lebron James Reveals His Top 5 Tips for Conquering Hard Work," YouTube, November 11, 2023, https://www.youtube.com/watch?v=f2xrJsEP82U.

As a young, single mom, life was hard for Gloria. But thankfully, she had support from her mother, with whom she and LeBron lived. Circumstances changed when LeBron was three and his grand-mother died, leaving Gloria to raise her son on her own again. Gloria struggled to provide for her young child. The family scraped by, living on government assistance, unable to afford necessities. Bills and expenses piled up, and Gloria could not pay them. They moved from place to place, but financial problems followed her wherever she went.

The constant movement and instability made it hard for LeBron to settle in or feel grounded as he got older. Without structure or discipline, LeBron often had to fend for himself, and his edu-cation took the biggest hit. He regularly skipped school because he lived too far away, had no means of transportation, or lacked motivation and encouragement. In fourth grade, he even missed eighty-three days of school. His mother tried to make things work, but life was difficult for her. She loved her son and wanted what was best for him, but things never worked out. LeBron understood and appreciated how hard his mom worked for them, and he loved her regardless of their situation.

While his home life was shaky, young LeBron had activities in life he enjoyed, like playing video games, watching TV, especially sports, and playing with neighborhood kids. One day, Bruce Kelker, coach of the East Dragons recreational football team, approached LeBron and his friends playing in the neighborhood and asked them if they wanted to join his team. The kids were eager to par-ticipate, and as it turned out, football would open a whole new world for LeBron.

LeBron enjoyed being a part of a team and loved playing football. Kelker took him under his wing, training him and providing a tem-porary home for LeBron and his mom. But when Kelker could no longer house them, another coach, Frankie Walker, stepped in and gave LeBron a place to live and the stability he needed.

The Walker household had three other children besides LeBron. LeBron fell in line with the Walker children and followed a daily routine of chores and schoolwork. Playing in his backyard net, Walker was the first to introduce basketball to LeBron when he was nine. LeBron took to the game easily and learned to play with confidence. Walker also taught him discipline and values and prioritized education in LeBron's life. With the support of a stable family, LeBron thrived in his athletic ability and also in school.

It was clear early on that LeBron was a natural in basketball. While still in middle school, he played for an AAU team called the Ohio Shooting Stars. He formed a strong friendship with three of his teammates, Sian Cotton, Dru Joyce III, and Willie McGee, which has lasted to this day. The group called themselves the "The Fab Four." They bonded over the game and aspired to win the national championships. They were good. Very good. And their performances on the court made them local names around town.

The Fab Four were excited when they learned the team qualified to enter the national championships. They worked and trained hard; it was all they could think about. The team made it all the way to the tournament in Orlando and reached the finals. But they lost the game by one point. Still, they had come so far and showed everyone who said they couldn't, that they could.

It was a defining moment for LeBron and his friends. And instead of feeling defeated by the loss, it fueled their desire even more. They had no intention of abandoning their dream; instead, they made a pact. They all agreed they would attend the same high school to play for the same basketball team and take that team to the championship win. It was expected that LeBron and his friends would go to the predominately Black school, John R. Buchtel Community Learning Center. But in a turn of events, the group ended up at St. Vincent-St. Mary (SVSM), a Catholic prep school that offered scholarships.

LeBron would later say of the school, "This is the place where all the dreams turned into reality. If you grow up poor and black in this country, you dream a lot, but you don't really think they're going to come true. This is where it all started—where I began to think I could do it."[26]

In high school, The Fab Four became "The Fab Five" with the addition of Romeo Travis. Together, the friends dominated high school basketball, with LeBron as a strong leader. And as they dreamed, they took the court by storm. The freshman led the way to put SVSM ahead of other teams with no losses and twenty-seven wins that season. In their first year, the friends already did what they said they would do and won the Division III state title. Things only got better from there.

The streak continued throughout LeBron's high school years, with SVSM dominating the competition. LeBron established himself as both a leader and a team player. And his consistently high scores were indicative of the basketball superstar he would become. SVSM won state championships three times under the command of LeBron and his friends.

As his basketball game progressed, so did his football game. LeBron was a star athlete in both sports, but football had been his first love ever since he was a kid. He had the build and stamina for the rough game of football and used it to his advantage. He was a

26 David Murphy, "21 People Who Made LeBron James the Man He Is Today," *Bleacher Report,* October 3, 2017, https://bleacherreport.com/articles/1876553 -21-people-who-made-lebron-james-the-man-he-is-today.

powerful wide receiver and helped his team make it to the state semifinals in his junior year. As a top prospect in both sports, he received a slew of offers from universities and colleges eager to give him full athletic scholarships. But LeBron realized he couldn't focus on both sports; the risk of injury would be too great. Ultimately, he decided on basketball and the dream of playing in the NBA.

LeBron exploded onto the media scene while still in high school. He was considered the best high school basketball player in the entire country. Often compared to Michael Jordan, LeBron was a phenom in his own right. And the fans and the media couldn't get enough. His story was even featured in the February 18, 2002, issue of *Sports Illustrated*. On the cover of the issue, a teenage LeBron grasped a basketball. And in bold white letters beside his image read the words, "The Chosen One." It was a bold label for a seventeen-year-old who had not yet finished high school. But the nickname stuck, and LeBron embraced it. Many speculated he had a bright future ahead of him, but no one could have foreseen just how bright it would be.

LeBron was as excited to get his professional career off the ground as everyone else. He was ready, or so he thought, to leave high school behind and join the NBA. But the NBA had strict rules. At seventeen, LeBron was too young for the draft. Although he petitioned the NBA to change their rules, they denied him. So, he deferred his dream for one more year. The delay only added to the growing excitement around which team would be lucky enough to land LeBron in the draft.

PATH TO SUCCESS

As it turns out, the Cleveland Cavaliers won the lottery on May 22, 2003, giving them the first pick on draft day. And there was one player at the top of their priority list: LeBron James. The Cavs couldn't believe their luck. And for LeBron, who was watching the televised lottery with family and friends, it was time to celebrate. "Everyone just started yelling and coming over to me and jumping on me. From then on, that night, it was a blur. I didn't even see them pull out the jersey with my name on it. I didn't see that until later," LeBron said in his recount of the day.

A little over a month later, on June 26, 2003, LeBron was officially drafted into the NBA. The event received plenty of media attention, as everyone was eager to see him and other talented players selected. LeBron was the number-one draft pick. Cleveland got their wish, and they hoped LeBron could bring life to a floundering team. For LeBron, it was the fulfillment of everything he had been working toward. "It was great. This is a longtime dream—to finally accomplish this," [27] James said. And to think it all started back with Coach Walker and the first time he picked up a basketball, and it intensified with The Fab Four and the quest for greatness.

The Cavs were eager to get hometown boy LeBron on board, and it meant a lot for him to play for the city and make his mom proud. Everyone in the basketball world eagerly awaited the debut of LeBron James to see if he, in fact, was the Chosen One.

The wait lasted four months before LeBron debuted as a Cavalier against the Sacramento Kings on October 29, 2003. And he more than lived up to the hype, scoring twenty-five points in his first game. But despite his efforts, Cleveland lost. It would take more than one night or one game to turn things around for the Cav-

---

27 Brian Windhorst, "In Their Own Words: How the Legendary 2003 NBA Draft Shaped Basketball's Future," ESPN, May 22, 2023, https://www.espn.com/nba/story/_/id/35799683/oral-history-2023-nba-draft-lottery-lebron-james-carmelo-anthony-chris-bosh-dwyane-wade.

aliers. LeBron knew this and was eager and willing to put in the work.

Over time, LeBron's addition to the team had a huge impact on the fortune of the Cavaliers. That season, they won thirty-three games and lost forty-seven, a vast improvement from the 17-65 record of the previous season. LeBron played hard and surpassed many expectations. But the Cavaliers were still struggling despite him pulling them out of their long-lasting slump and helping them win more games than they had in previous years. In a 2004 game against the New Jersey Nets, he even scored a whopping forty-one points. While it was his career-best at the time, it also set a new NBA record. LeBron was now the youngest player to score over forty points in a game. On average, LeBron scored twenty points and five assists in his rookie year. And for his accomplishments on the court, he was named Rookie of the Year, showing that he wasn't all hype but a force to be reckoned with.

But it would take more than one year to make the Cavaliers serious contenders for the championship. And LeBron was up for the challenge.

LeBron continued to dazzle during his time with the Cavs. In his second year, he was voted to the All-Star NBA team, making him the second-youngest player to do so. That game also marked another milestone for LeBron when he was awarded the All-Star game MVP title. At twenty-one years old, he was the youngest player to win the award.

With LeBron anchoring the Cavaliers, the team steadily improved. Their wins outnumbered their losses year after year. But they had yet to make it to the playoffs. The Cavs hadn't been in the playoffs since 1998. Seven long years had passed, and everyone wondered if LeBron would be the one to change their fortune. He wanted to be.

In his third season with the Cavs, LeBron averaged thirty-one points per game. And he showed he could do much more, sometimes scoring upwards of forty points. He even broke the record for the Cavaliers' all-time leading scorer. His hard work and determination paid off. That year, the Cavs made it to the NBA playoffs. It was a massive accomplishment for LeBron and the team.

The Eastern Conference saw the Cavs face off against the Detroit Pistons in the finals. The Cavaliers won the series over the Pistons, leading them to the much-anticipated NBA finals and a chance at the championship. But the Cavs lost the series to the San Antonio Spurs. The championship wouldn't be theirs after all, but LeBron had brought them closer than they had been in years.

In his time with the Cavs, LeBron carried the team. They had moved from ninth place in the Eastern Conference in his rookie year to first place by the time he left in 2010. LeBron brought them to five Eastern Conference playoffs, two semifinals, and one finals series. But no matter how close they got, the championship remained out of reach.

Aside from the regular season, LeBron continued to rack up achievements. He played for the Olympic team at the Beijing 2008 Summer Olympic Games and was in good company with Kobe Bryant, Dwayne Wade, and other basketball superstars. They won against Spain in the finals, bringing the Olympic gold home to the US. And they would repeat the win in the 2012 Olympic Games in London.

TRIALS AND TRIBULATIONS

In 2010, after seven years with the Cavs, LeBron became a free agent. He longed to be a championship winner, but his dreams had not come true in all his years with the Cavs. He knew something had to change. But what? The basketball world anxiously waited to see what his next move would be. Would he stay with the Cavs and continue to build the team, or would he part ways with Cleveland in pursuit of an NBA title?

In the end, he signed with the Miami Heat. The Heat already had superstar players Dwyane Wade and Chris Bosh, powerhouse athletes who ruled the court. By joining Miami, LeBron banked on forming an unstoppable team to guarantee a championship. His decision was met with criticism and disappointment from critics and fans. Before LeBron's move to Miami, players typically remained with a team for their entire basketball career unless they were traded or experienced injuries. LeBron did things differently. Many believed his sole motivation was winning a championship, and he abandoned the team when they needed him most.

LeBron, who started as a media darling, soon discovered this decision would completely change his reputation. Suddenly, people on all sides questioned him and wondered if he had any loyalty. Many felt he owed it to Cleveland to stay and continue to build the team. Others thought it was selfish of him to join an already powerful team for the sole purpose of winning.

It was an emotional decision for LeBron; playing for Cleveland had meant a lot to him. But he also saw it as a strategic move that could catapult his career. He was on a mission to build a dynasty. He didn't allow the backlash to hold him back or alter his mindset. Drawing from the adversity, he declared, "I play the game of basketball with a lot of love. A lot of passion. . . . I can't worry about what everybody says about me. I'm LeBron James from Akron,

Ohio, from the inner city. I'm not even supposed to be here. That's enough. Every night I walk into the locker room, I see a number six with James on the back, and I'm blessed."[28]

But things had changed. Where he was once called confident, he was now called cocky; he was booed at games, and the media was quick to chronicle his declining popularity. He envisioned winning many championships with the Heat and said as much, but his proclamation only made the dislike grow. Instead of fighting the new persona the media created of him, he accepted it and oftentimes played into it.

But winning was more challenging than he thought it was going to be. LeBron debuted with the Heat on October 26, 2010. And while he scored thirty-one points, the Heat lost the game. It wasn't a great start. It was apparent this new super team needed time to adjust. But the team found their groove later in the season, and LeBron, along with Wade and Bosh, made it to the NBA playoffs, as he had hoped.

While they made it to the finals, they suffered a crushing loss against the Dallas Mavericks, with LeBron scoring an all-time low of just eight points in one game. The team still needed some tweaking. Critics were quick to say the defeat showed that LeBron didn't have what it took to win a championship; he could lead a team to the finals but could not deliver a win. LeBron knew, too, that a lot more work needed to be done before they could win a championship.

The loss only intensified LeBron's desire, like it did in the days of the Fab Four. And he was determined to do whatever he could to become a championship winner. He placed a great emphasis on

---

28 EntreXpreneur, "This Is Lebron James | Motivation from LeBron James," YouTube, December 27, 2021, https://www.youtube.com/watch?v=4DfVOHaD67A.

training, practice, and remaining in good shape. He followed a rigorous diet and exercise program and looked to fellow mentors for advice. And those changes marked a turning point in his career.

ACHIEVEMENTS

In the 2011–2012 season, LeBron returned with a mission to bring home a trophy for himself and Miami. He averaged twenty-seven points in the season, and the team won forty-six of sixty-six games. There was no doubt they would make it to the playoffs, but could they emerge with the title they desperately wanted?

In the hard-fought finals game on June 5, 2012, against the Oklahoma City Thunder, the Heat won the series. Finally, LeBron had his championship win, and what a great day it was. LeBron also won the Finals MVP award for his performance in the series. For LeBron, this was the culmination of everything he had ever wanted. And it silenced his critics.

LeBron played with Miami for four seasons, from 2010 to 2014. And he made it to the championships every year he was with the Heat. The year following their 2012 win, the Heat won another championship title. Two consecutive championship titles made it clear that LeBron was a man who delivered on his promises.

In a surprising twist, LeBron left Miami and returned to Cleveland at the end of his contract with the Heat. Cleveland had never won a professional championship, and LeBron was determined to change that. Cleveland was ready to forgive LeBron, and all anybody wanted to know was, could he do for the Cavs what he had done for the Heat? He promised Cleveland a championship title, and all he had to do was make good on that promise. In 2015, a capacity stadium of twenty thousand fans welcomed LeBron back to his first game in Cleveland. It was a triumphant return to the city.

And in 2016, Lebron fulfilled his promise to the city, giving the Cavs their first championship win in the final game against the Golden State Warriors. LeBron was ecstatic. "This is the happiest time in my life right now,"[29] he said.

With a promise kept, LeBron would stay on with the Cavs for only two more years, leaving Cleveland for the LA Lakers in 2018. In LA, LeBron and the Lakers won another championship title against the Miami Heat. Four championship titles with three different teams put LeBron in an exclusive group. Only three other players have achieved this accomplishment.

While championship titles are by far the greatest of his achievements, he's amassed many other awards and broken many records in his basketball career. Some of these include being selected for and playing in nineteen All-Star games. He has won the NBA MVP award four times and the All-Star Games MVP award three times. He's the only player in the NBA to win the finals MVP award on three different teams.

He is the NBA's new all-time scoring leader, a feat he achieved on February 7, 2023, when he reached 38,390, surpassing Kareem Abdul-Jabbar's long-standing record.

Playing for Team USA in basketball, LeBron is a three-time Olympic medalist, with two gold medals and one bronze medal.

---

29 "LeBron James Staying with the Cavaliers: 'I Love It Here in Cleveland,'" *The Guardian*, June 23, 2016, https://www.theguardian.com/sport/2016/jun/22/lebron-james-staying-cleveland-cavaliers-nba.

LIFE LESSONS

With a career that's lasted nearly twenty years, LeBron James is considered one of basketball's best and most gifted players. He has shown he can adapt to any situation and come out a winner. When people questioned his decisions, he stayed true to himself and his goals, knowing his reasoning was sound. And most importantly, he followed through with his intentions and honored his promises.

He is undoubtedly a dominating presence on the court with a six foot, nine-inch frame, but it takes more than physique or natural skills to get you to where LeBron is. It takes steely determination and a never-quit attitude.

"At the end of my career when I hang up my jersey, and you guys see it in the rafters—whatever arena it's in—you guys can say he made a mark on this game,"[30] LeBron said of his contributions to the game.

And he would be right. Whether you think he's the greatest of all time or not, you cannot dispute LeBron's passion and dedication to the game. He has played every position on the team, showcasing his versatility and exceptional performance. He works hard and practices daily to remain an elite player. Of course, it's not easy, but reaching for your dreams takes commitment and dedication. He has brought the teams on which he has played to some of the highest highs, sometimes as a leader and always as a team player.

---

30 Grant Hughes, "How LeBron James Can Fulfill His Dream of Being NBA's Greatest Ever," *Bleacher Report,* September 22, 2017, https://bleacherreport. com/articles/1745816-how-lebron-james-can-fulfill-his-dream-of-being-nbas -greatest-ever.

LeBron has shown that if you want something, you have to go after it, you have to work for it, and you can't be afraid to fail. Although he may have nothing left to prove, LeBron, who turns forty in 2024, still remains ready to lace up his shoes. And he may break a few more records yet.

EARL FRANCIS LLOYD

> "... In any life there's going to be adversity, and you're going to have to develop real character, or you won't be able to overcome your troubles. All the skills in the world, all the wonderful gifts and characteristics, they mean absolutely nothing if you're not courageous. Courage doesn't mean being unafraid. Courage means being afraid, and going ahead anyway." [31]

EARLY YEARS

The first African American to play in the NBA was as shocked as anyone else to find out he was drafted into the pros. Playing professional basketball was the last thing on his mind. But when the opportunity came calling, Earl Francis Lloyd answered. It was a step that would take his life down an unexpected and historic path.

Born in the segregated South on April 3, 1928, Earl Francis Lloyd came from humble beginnings. His mother, Daisy Mitchell Lloyd, was a maid, and his father, Theodore Lloyd, shoveled coal at the coal yards. They worked relentlessly at their exhausting, physically demanding jobs to support their family. Their tireless examples imprinted the value of a strong work ethic on Earl and his older brothers, Ernest and Ted.

---

31 Earl Lloyd and Sean Peter Kirst, *Moonfixer: The Basketball Journey of Earl Lloyd* (Syracuse, NY: Syracuse University Press, 2011).

Earl's family didn't have a lot, but they had what they needed. Their parents made sure their children didn't want for anything, and there was always an abundance of love in the Lloyd household. When Earl was young, his family moved to a new development in the projects. Although project housing came with problems, it was an upgrade from the small, rundown house they had been living in, which didn't even have plumbing. In the new development, at least, Earl had his room and was thankful for that.

The family lived in Alexandria, Virginia, in a rough part of town designated for African Americans. For Earl and other Black people, life in Alexandria was far from ideal. Whites and Blacks lived separate lives, divided by the rules of segregation that were strictly enforced. Life was especially hard for Black youths. Denied access to the same activities and opportunities as the white children, they had little to preoccupy themselves. There were no part-time jobs, no organized activities, and no recreational facilities or places where they could hang out. It was a gloomy situation.

Despite the despair and limitations of segregation, Earl's parents raised their children to have confidence. In a world that told Black people their value was less than others, his mother encouraged Earl and his brothers to believe in themselves. Earl's mother was his greatest influence, and she helped him believe in his worth.

His parents knew education was the key to escaping a life of limited possibilities like theirs. So, they instilled in their children a respect for teachers and authority. And Earl was fortunate enough to have had great teachers, mentors, and coaches who guided him throughout his life.

Sports became a natural outlet for many kids like Earl because there was little else for them to do in the city. Growing up, Earl and his friends played softball, football, and basketball. But his favorites were softball and basketball.

Earl went to Lyles-Crouch Elementary School and was a good student, even skipping grade six. But it was also in middle school that Earl became aware of the sense of hopelessness with which most people viewed the disparity of segregation. These injustices made him angry, and it would have been easy to fall into despair, too. But with the help of his teachers and parents, Earl excelled at school and had the chance at a future that many other children did not.

When Earl moved on to high school, he found little change. Resources were sub-par, even here. He attended Parker-Gray High School, the designated school for Black students. Everything from the books to the building itself was below the standards of the white schools or was lacking altogether. His school didn't even have a gym, a track, or a field to play on. The disparity between the Black and white sections of the city made him resentful and sad.

Despite the inadequacies of the school, Earl was an excellent student and athlete. He was a star player on the basketball team. He was a powerful player with his towering six-foot, seven-inch frame, earning nicknames like "Big Cat" and "Moonfixer." Earl was named three times to the All-South Atlantic Conference, the annual conference basketball championship tournament for the South Atlantic states, and the All-State Virginia Interscholastic Conference twice, where the best high school players in the state competed.

His ability on the court paid off. In 1946, he graduated from high school and received a scholarship to West Virginia State University. He was the first person in his family to go to college, and he knew there would be no discussion on whether he was going.

This opportunity was what his parents had hoped for and the reason he had worked so hard. The all-Black college was a revelation for Earl. He was in his element, surrounded by people who looked like him, pursuing higher education, following their goals, and discovering their freedom away from home and the restrictions of segregation. He enjoyed his college years from 1946–1950. In that time, he grew as both a person and a player.

In college, he played basketball for the West Virginia State Yellow Jackets and proved to be an outstanding athlete. In the 1947–48 season, the team went undefeated. That year, they made it to the Central Intercollegiate Athletic Conference (CIAA) and won the championship. They retook the CIAA championship the following year. Earl was named All-American twice and earned the All-Conference title three times during college.

Sports at Black colleges received little mainstream press back then, but word had gotten out about the Yellow Jackets' performance. It caught the attention of a promoter, who offered them a chance to come to California and play against other top-rated white collegiate teams.

It was an exciting opportunity that signified things were slowly changing in basketball. The team lost their first game against St. Mary's but won against Santa Clara. In the end, they lost more games than they won. But the experience gave them a new confidence that showed they were on the same level as any other team, Black or white.

Plus, someone who would significantly impact the direction of Earl's life was watching one of these college tournaments.

PATH TO SUCCESS

In his senior year of college, the most surprising thing happened to Earl. He got drafted into the NBA. He wasn't expecting it, nor did he know how it happened. In fact, he wasn't even informed! He found out through a friend who'd heard the news on the radio. Imagine his surprise. This new development would take him far off the track he had envisioned for himself. He'd originally wanted to be a teacher or a coach to give back to the community that had done so much for him. But Earl, never one to let an opportunity pass him by, counted his blessings and seized the opportunity.

Albert "Bones" McKinney, coach of the Washington Capitols, was the one who caught sight of Earl at the college tournament earlier that year. He was so impressed by what he saw that he took a chance on Earl and selected him to be on his team.

Earl was chosen as a ninth-round draft pick by the Washington Capitols, one of the originating teams in the NBA. He was pick number one hundred for the Capitols. Earl was way down on the roster, but then again, he hadn't even known he was in the running, so the placement didn't bother him. Earl knew he would make his mark, no matter where or how he started.

Just like that, Earl's life was suddenly headed in a completely different direction than he had planned. It was daunting and scary but also exciting. He was eager to start tryouts in Washington.

Interestingly, Earl wasn't the first African American drafted into the NBA. There was also Chuck Cooper, a second-round draft pick in 1950, and Nat "Sweetwater" Clifton, a first-round pick. Cooper was chosen to play for the Boston Celtics and Clifton for the New York Knicks. So how did Earl become the first Black player in the NBA when others were drafted ahead of him? The answer is as simple as scheduling. The season started in November for the Knicks and the Celtics. Meanwhile, Earl made his NBA debut in October.

After the tryouts, Earl was excited to learn he'd made the final starting team. But he wasn't the only Black player selected by the Washington Capitols in that draft. Harold Hunter, who was also selected, had to be dropped from the team early on. In the racially charged climate of 1950, there was barely a place for one Black player, let alone two. That was unheard of.

It was overwhelming for Earl at first. Though the opportunity was exciting, he couldn't help but expect the worst and for segregation to divide the team. He was uncomfortable in this new social situation. He hadn't been around many white people in his life, let alone played on a team with them. However, by keeping an open mind and giving 100 percent to the team, he slowly developed a sense of belonging as he trained and practiced with his fellow players. Eventually, his doubts began to disappear.

He found that his skin color didn't matter to his teammates, at least while they were on the court. While they were playing, everyone had the same objective: to win. "I also knew if I was going to compete with these guys, that you can't be just good. To get somebody's attention, you've got to be better. I accepted that; it became my mantra, and it drove me,"[32] Earl said of his starting days with the team.

Earl's professional debut came on October 31, 1950, in a game against the Rochester Royals. He was off to a good start, scoring six points in the historic game the Royals won. But unlike the media frenzy that met Jackie Robinson when he broke the color line in baseball in 1947, the media didn't even note Earl's significant initiation into the pros. At the time, baseball was still America's

---

32 Lloyd and Kirst, *Moonfixer*.

favorite pastime, and professional basketball was still finding its way.

Despite Earl's strong start, his time with the Capitols was cut short. He played with them for only seven games before the struggling team folded in early 1951. But another event would shift his focus from the NBA. Earl was drafted into the Army and fought in the Korean War. But even in the military, he played basketball, earning four Army basketball championships during his service. Meanwhile, back at home, the players from the defunct Washington team were placed into another draft, and the Syracuse Nationals selected Earl.

Fresh out of the Army, Earl joined the Nationals in 1952. And it was in Syracuse that Earl would make a name for himself. In college, he had been a top scorer. But Syracuse already had high scorers—white scorers. Therefore, Earl was told there wasn't room for him to hold this position, too. Replacing a white player with a Black player just wasn't done at the time. He was asked to become a forward instead and protect the top scorers on the team. Though Earl understood this reasoning, he still felt hurt by the injustice of it. Nevertheless, he took on his new role as guard with the same commitment and energy he always had.

Known for his powerful defensive work and accurate rebounding, Earl was a solid addition to the team. In the 1952–53 and the 1954–55 seasons, the Nationals finished second in the NBA Eastern Division. While they made it to the playoffs in 1953, they only got as far as the semifinals, where they lost to the Boston Celtics. They were at the playoffs again in 1954, and this time, the Nationals made it to the NBA championships finals, where they faced the Minneapolis Lakers. The series lasted for seven games, but in the end, they lost to the Lakers in a close final match.

The following year, the Nationals won the Eastern division, placing them back at the NBA championship finals. This time, they faced the Fort Wayne Pistons. Earl averaged nine points in the seven-game series. It was a hard-fought series, and the Nationals won the final game by one point, with 91-92 being the final score. The Nationals had claimed the crown as the 1955 NBA champions. In so doing, Earl became the first Black man to win an NBA Championship. Dolph Schayes, Earl's former teammate, would later say of Earl's contribution to the game, "Without Earl, we never would have won the title. Earl was the guy who covered the other team's best player, and his strengths were rebounding, defense, and battling the boards."[33]

Earl played with the Nationals for six seasons before they traded him to the Detroit Pistons in 1958. In his time with Syracuse, he was a strong player, averaging twenty-six minutes on the court, eight points, and six rebounds per game.

TRIALS AND TRIBULATIONS

Until he reached university, Earl had little interaction with white people. He was used to his all-Black neighborhood and his all-Black classmates at school. Growing up in the segregation era, he knew there were places where he could and could not go, as much for his safety as it was against the law. So, it made sense for him to avoid white spaces.

He could never understand the separate but equal philosophy of segregation. And he would never forget how segregation made him feel. Though his parents and mentors taught Earl to believe

---

33 Bill Dow, "Former Piston Earl Lloyd Recalls Breaking the NBA Color Barrier," Vintage Detroit Collection, February 28, 2015, https://www.vintagedetroit.com /former-piston-earl-lloyd-recalls-breaking-the-nba-color-barrier.

in himself, throughout moments in his life, he would often feel "othered"—like he didn't belong.

Even though he had no racist interactions with other players, the same couldn't be said for those who attended the games. He encountered opposition from fans and critics who weren't shy about showing their displeasure that he was on the team. He was the target of racist jeers, name-calling, and boos when he was on court. And in many cities, he wasn't allowed to eat in the same restaurants or stay in the same hotels as his team members.

It left him feeling demoralized. In one particular incident, an opposing team barred him from playing an exhibition game with the rest of his team in Greenville, South Carolina. While he knew the team had to go forward with the game, he expected at least one of his teammates to acknowledge how unjust the barring was. But no one ever did. This oversight hurt him. He realized that people would always consider him "the other," which made him feel alone.

And even though he had some of his best years with Syracuse, he was an equal only on the court. Like other Black people in Syracuse, he had to live in a specific area of town. He existed in two worlds; he worked with white people and lived with Black people.

But if his mother had taught him anything, it was how to persevere in difficult situations. He worked hard to ensure his resentment and anger didn't overwhelm him and stop him from excelling in his career. He never wanted to allow anyone to say he wasn't good enough or couldn't withstand the pressure.

Above all, as the first Black man in the NBA, he always felt a tremendous responsibility to the kids and other Black athletes watching him. He was determined to succeed for their sake as much as his own. And he also felt responsible to the people who helped raise and guide him: his parents, teachers, coaches, and elders who believed in him. He knew he couldn't let them down. They all played a part in how far he had come.

ACHIEVEMENTS

Earl was traded to Detroit in 1958—a city he would grow to love and call home. He played with the Detroit Pistons for two seasons, from 1958–1960. Dick McGuire, who had been his teammate just the year before in the 1959 season, was hired for the position of coach. McGuire offered Earl the position of scout and assistant coach. Earl didn't know if he was ready to give up basketball. He was only thirty-two years old. But the game was changing, and bigger and better players were coming up in the league.

Earl accepted the job. The offer meant a lot to him, especially considering everything he'd been through as a Black man. To be recognized for his abilities and skills and not the color of his skin meant the world to him.

As a scout, Earl had the job of finding fresh, young players for the team. It was a full-circle moment for him. He now had the chance to provide opportunities, like the one he had received, to players. And as an assistant coach, he had a hand in building the team. Earl was the NBA's first Black assistant coach.

He stayed in the position for eight years. In 1968, he left basketball for a corporate job with the Chrysler Corporation. But basketball wasn't finished with Earl yet. In 1971, the Detroit Pistons asked him to return to be the head coach of the team.

They offered him a two-year contract, and he had no doubts about taking the job. He was eager to give back to the team and felt honored that they'd called on him. The position would mark another first for Earl. Before 1985, it was common for a coach to play and coach simultaneously. Earl was the first non-playing Black coach in the NBA. He then hired Ray Scott as his assistant coach, and together, they were one of the first all-Black coaching teams.

Earl made his mark as the first African American in the NBA. He worked hard and came to play in every game. He contributed to the success of his teams and the advancement of Black athletes in sports.

As a player, his professional career lasted nine years, during which he played 560 games. He won the NBA championship in 1955 with his Syracuse teammates, making him the first Black man to win a championship. And he continued to trailblaze as an assistant and head coach of an NBA team.

Earl was inducted into the Naismith Memorial Basketball Hall of Fame in 2003 for his great contributions.

LIFE LESSONS

Earl's death on February 26, 2015, marked the end of a remarkable life. He had lived through the oppression of segregation and made it to the heights of professional success.

Just three years before Earl joined the Washington Capitols, Jackie Robinson had done the impossible. He had penetrated the deeply segregated world of professional baseball. Jackie was the first Black man to play for a major league team, defying the odds and the opposition. Earl watched that history unfold like so many others and knew what it would mean for Black athletes in sports. But he did not know he would also become an important part of history.

Earl was often compared to Jackie. But it was a comparison he didn't accept. In his mind, Jackie's entry into professional baseball was difficult and dangerous. Jackie overcame verbal and physical attacks, threats, and criticism on all fronts without caving to the pressure. At the time, everyone was invested in the outcome of Jackie's situation, specifically how he would conduct himself in such a volatile atmosphere. Everything was riding on Jackie's ability to persevere. If he succeeded and was accepted into baseball, there was a good chance it would open the door for Black athletes in other sports.

Earl recognized that basketball in the 1950s didn't have the same attraction as baseball, and integration wasn't as volatile. The eyes of the nation weren't on Earl the way they had been on Jackie. And Earl was thankful for that. He was able to concentrate on doing his best and playing the game.

So, what life lessons can we take from Earl's inspirational story? We can start with the importance of showing up for yourself and others, opening yourself to new experiences, putting forth your best effort, and rising above adversity. But most of all, it can teach us to have courage even when we're afraid. Because Earl had the courage to pursue the opportunities that came his way, he became a part of history and lived a remarkable life—a life so different from the one he grew up in.

Earl had the perseverance and courage to follow through, but he also knew he didn't get there on his own. "From the time I started school, I had people I believed in, people who loved me, who were telling me there was a way to succeed. I was a Black kid born in Virginia in 1928. My prospects were slim and none, and here I am."[34] Earl was always thankful for the people he met along the way and their impact on his life. He knew he couldn't have gotten as far as he did without their intervention and help. His story

---

34 Lloyd and Kirst, *Moonfixer*.

reminds us to be grateful for our opportunities and those who had a hand in getting us to our dreams.

While Earl's accomplishments were quietly marked in the pages of history, they nevertheless helped pave the way for others who would come after him. And for that, he should be remembered.

CHAPTER 4

FOOTBALL

RUSSELL WILSON AND FRITZ POLLARD

RUSSELL WILSON

"There's a difference between just being successful and being significant. My goal is to be significant. My goal is to make a difference, to do it better than anybody's ever done it." [35]

EARLY YEARS

In the game of football, the quarterback reigns supreme. Responsible for leading the offense and engineering plays, the quarterback is the backbone of any NFL team. What separates a great quarterback from a good one is how they use their mental and physical abilities to control the game and command their players. Russell Wilson, considered one of the sport's best quarterbacks, is the complete package and more. As one of only three Black quarterbacks to win a Super Bowl, Russell has cemented his place in NFL history.

Russell Carrington Wilson is the middle child born to lawyer Harrison Wilson III and nurse Tammy Wilson. Russell's older brother is Harrison IV, and his younger sister is Anna. Russell was born in Cincinnati, Ohio, on November 29, 1988, but when he was a year old, the family moved to Richmond, Virginia, after his father accepted a new job there.

---

[35] Steve Rudman, "Super Bowl Interception Still Haunts Wilson," *Sportspress Northwest*, February 20, 2015, https://www.sportspressnw.com/2198735/2015/wilson-steps-up-takes-blame-for-super-bowl-loss.

Russell comes from a long line of achievers with a diverse ancestry, including a famous painter, a university president, a former slave who fought for her freedom, and a European saint with links to a Frankish king. Success runs in his blood. But for Russell, the most important people in his life were his parents. Their value systems and teachings would greatly influence his personal success.

The Wilsons provided their children with a loving, stable home filled with encouragement. Faith and religion were a high priority in the Wilson household, and they attended church every Sunday and instilled in their children a strong belief in God.

Russell was an active kid who, growing up, always had a ball in his hand and played many sports with his friends and family. He started playing baseball in his grandfather's backyard when he was just two or three. He loved the sport, and eventually, it grew into a passion. He started playing football a little later, at four years old. Roughhousing around the house with his brother and father while tossing the football are some of Russell's fondest memories. He also liked shooting hoops with his brother in their backyard. He and his brother were very competitive, and like most younger siblings, Russell always wanted to beat his brother in whatever game they played.

Russell was a member of a local little league baseball team but only joined a football league when he was in middle school. The Tuckahoe Tomahawks was his first football team; from the beginning, he displayed a natural ability. On his second day with the team, they unexpectedly threw him into the mid-season game as a replacement for an injured player. He immediately worked out plays, navigated the opposition, and led the team to a win.

Russell's parents felt as strongly about education as they did about religion. And while the Wilsons supported and encouraged their children to play sports, athletics always came second to education. The children had to maintain good grades if they wanted to pursue athletics. And Russell, who loved sports, made sure to comply.

Russell's father was a former collegiate football player who understood the value of sports and education. He always motivated Russell to do his best in everything he did. Wilson credits his parents with teaching him the importance of dedication and commitment and says, "They always encouraged me, and that was the most important thing. They gave me a greater vision than even my own. They allowed me to have an imagination."[36] His parents allowed him to dream big and told him anything was within his reach if he worked for it. And Russell had big dreams.

With their stance on education being what it was, Russell attended Collegiate School, a private preparatory school in Richmond, from elementary to high school.

While at Collegiate, Russell took part in many team sports. From very early on, he proved he was a team player, quick learner, and thoughtful leader with an insatiable drive to succeed—all elements that make for a great athlete.

As a kid, Russell fantasized about where his athletic pursuits would take him. He knew his God-given talents would lead him to success; it was just a matter of time. "I always dreamed of playing big-time football and baseball, making it to the NFL, and making it to the major leagues. I just didn't know where I'd end up,"[37] Russell once said. He had lofty goals, but Russell believed he could do it.

---

36 The Richmond Forum, "Russell Wilson with Dr. Henry Louis Gates, Jr. At the Richmond Forum," YouTube, April 18, 2016, https://www.youtube.com /watch?v=4aZCBlL8P6U.

37 "Parting Words from Russell Wilson," Collegiate School, July 13, 2007, https://www.collegiate-va.org/news-detail?pk=399055.

As a multitalented athlete, Russell divided his time in high school between baseball and football and did exceptionally well in both. His batting average as a junior was an outstanding .467. In his final year, the Baltimore Orioles picked him in the forty-first round of the draft. But turning pro out of high school was not a part of Russell's or his parents' plan. College came first.

Despite his strides in baseball, Russell's most noteworthy performances came on the gridiron.

In football, a quarterback's success is measured by how many passing yards, touchdown passes, and pass completions they achieve. And even as a teen, Russell could put up impressive numbers in those areas. In his junior year, he threw 3,287 yards and had 40 touchdown passes, leading his team to an 11-0 record that season and earning him the Richmond Times-Dispatch Player of the Year. Russell's leadership resulted in three state championships for the team from 2004 to 2006. Outstanding achievements marked Russell's senior year as he threw for 3,009 yards and 34 passing touchdowns, earning him the titles of all-conference and all-state. He was also named Conference Player of the Year and featured in *Sports Illustrated* as an athlete to watch.

He had all the makings of a star football player: a keen understanding of the game, an ability to strategize, impressive throwing accuracy, and a knack for staying calm under pressure.

His performance in high school caught the eye of many college scouts, and he toured many campuses to find the one that would be the right fit for him. But after touring North Carolina (NC) State University, Russell knew his search was over. Plus, he wanted to stay closer to home. His father had recently become ill, and Russell wanted to be close by. In 2006, Russell committed to NC State. He liked that he could pursue both sports at NC State because he wasn't ready to choose.

NC State proposed that Russell could be the starting quarterback, but he'd have to prove he could handle the job. With the unique opportunity to start in his freshman year ahead of him, Russell hit the playbooks. He studied them hard and trained hard. He was determined not to let this chance slip out of his hands. In the pre-season training, he outplayed Harrison Beck, the previous year's starting quarterback, and won the job.

Playing both baseball and football in college made for a busy schedule, especially as Russell had a full academic load, but he knew he could play both sports without sacrificing his performance. And he was right. But, while the setup worked well the first few years, it ultimately led to a conflict that would shift his college career.

In football, Russell was blazing a trail as a skilled quarterback. He started his junior year off with a bang, earning all-Atlantic Coast Conference (ACC) first-team honors, the first freshman to do so. In 2009, he achieved a streak of 379 passes without an interception, breaking the National Collegiate Athletic Association (NCAA) record.

Russell was a strong baseball player, too, averaging .282 over three years with North Carolina. In 2010, the Colorado Rockies drafted him in the fourth round. He accepted. Like all rookies, Russell began his baseball career in the minor leagues, hoping to work his way up to the pros. The first team on which he played within the Rockies franchise was the Tri-City Dust Devils, and then he moved up to the Asheville Tourists a year later.

Russell wanted to return to NC State for his senior year, but he was told by the football coach he wouldn't be able to come back to his starting quarterback position. Russell was devastated. The conflict resulted in Russell leaving NC State. He bounced back quickly, transferring to the University of Wisconsin (U of W) in 2010, where he would start as quarterback for the Badgers.

Choosing to concentrate solely on football, Wilson did not pursue baseball at U of W. He brought the same energy he always had to the game. His leadership led the team to win the Big Ten Conference Championship and compete in the Rose Bowl. After his momentous year at U of W, he was eager to enter the NFL draft. But where would he end up? It was the one question on Russell's mind and everyone else's as well.

PATH TO SUCCESS

In 2012, Russell made the tough decision to pursue professional football exclusively. In the 2012 draft, the Seattle Seahawks chose Russell as their seventy-fifth pick in the third round. While he wasn't a first-round draft pick, it was the beginning of what would be a phenomenal career. Russell was ecstatic to finally live out another one of his dreams and become a pro football player, especially after so many doubted he would be a contender.

Russell began his rookie year in contention for the quarterback position against Matt Flynn. Coach Pete Carroll had the two contenders show him what they could do on the field. And Russell, as always, came to impress. Carroll didn't need to look further when he saw how well Russell performed. In July, the coach selected Russell as the starting quarterback for the rest of the preseason and the regular season. Russell was thrilled. The next year, and every year after, Russell was the starting quarterback for the Seahawks.

Russell debuted in his first NFL season game on September 9, 2012, against the Arizona Cardinals. He unfortunately didn't have his best performance, and the team lost the game 20-16. Nevertheless, it was only up from there for Russell. The following week, on September 16, Russell showed he, indeed, was the right person for the job. The Seahawks overwhelmed the Dallas Cowboys, beating them 27-7.

The Seahawks finished the season strong, with Russell leading them to an 11-5 record that year. But Russell's first year is most prominently marked by what he could achieve as a rookie. He threw for 3,118 yards and twenty-six touchdowns, which tied him for the record for most touchdown passes by a rookie.

By 2013, with Russell at the helm, the Seahawks became the number-one team in the Northern Football Conference (NFC) with a 13-3 record, setting the stage for a triumphant season ahead.

The following year, 2014, was a stellar year that saw Russell throw twenty-six touchdown passes. The team's efforts culminated in a finals showdown with the Denver Broncos at the Super Bowl. The team dominated the game with a final score of 43-8, winning the championship and securing Seattle's first and only Super Bowl win.

The next year, 2015, the Seahawks made it to the NFC championship, battling against the Green Bay Packers for a spot in the Super Bowl. While it was a rough start for the Seahawks, who scored no points in the first half, they turned things around in the fourth quarter with a tied game. The game was forced into overtime, and Russell surprised everyone with a brilliant play that came just in time, resulting in a winning touchdown pass. The Seahawks won 28-22. It was a game that would go down in Seattle history as the day that Russell saved. The Seahawks were on their way to another Super Bowl! Russell broke down in tears, thankful they could make a triumphant turnaround.

But they wouldn't be so lucky in the following Super Bowl game, where they faced the New England Patriots. In a close game that came down to seconds on the clock, the Patriots defeated the Seahawks 28-24 after intercepting Russell's pass at the goal line. Russell, though devastated, remained confident that the team would be back in the Super Bowl.

His positive attitude and superior quarterbacking skills carried the team through five more seasons. Russell led the team to four more playoffs.

In 2019, Russell signed a contract extension with Seattle, which made him the highest-paid football player in the NFL. That year he finished with 4,110 passing yards and thirty-one passing touchdowns.

TRIALS AND TRIBULATIONS

At five feet, eleven inches, Russell is one of the shortest quarterbacks in the NFL. Because of his height, many doubted whether he would make it to the pros at all. As he waited to see if he would be drafted after college, critics speculated that his height would be his downfall and deter teams from choosing him. Many believed he would be better off playing baseball.

Can height make much of a difference? While five foot eleven doesn't sound short to the average person, a few extra inches can make a difference in football. The average football player is six feet, three inches, with long throwing arms. That additional height helps quarterbacks see far afield and over other players' heads. Russell didn't fit the mold, but he never doubted he could play the game better than other taller quarterbacks. Confident in his abilities, Russell knew football was where he wanted to be.

When the Seahawks took a chance on him, it allowed him to prove that he was not only a good quarterback but could be one of the best. "I think for me, it wasn't about proving people wrong; I think I was just proving myself right,"[38] Russell said.

Interestingly, Russell's height helped further distinguish him in the sport, as he became the shortest quarterback to win a Super Bowl Championship.

One of the biggest adversities Russell faced was the death of his father. In 2007, Russell's father had a stroke. At the time, his father wasn't expected to survive, but he managed to battle back even though physically he was never the same. But in June 2010, his father died from health complications.

Russell was a junior at NC State when it happened. And just the day before, the Colorado Rockies had drafted him as a fourth-round draft pick. One can only imagine the turmoil he must have felt.

All his life, Russell's father had been his greatest inspiration. Even after his stroke, his father was always there for Russell, showing up at his games and offering advice. He was the one who instilled in Russell the belief he could achieve anything. As Russell recalls, his father would often ask him, "'Son, *why not you*? Why don't you play pro baseball? Why don't you play pro football?' The idea of 'Why not you?' was really at the center of who I was. I started really subconsciously and consciously asking myself that question."[39] His

38 James Brown and Alvin Patrick, "Russell Wilson: The Seattle Seahawks Quarterback Wants to Have an Impact on Youth Far Beyond the Gridiron," *CBS News*, September 8, 2019, https://www.cbsnews.com/news/seattle-seahawks-qb -russell-wilson-why-not-you.

39 Brady Henderson, "'Why Not You?' Late Father Still Inspires Seattle Seahawks' Russell Wilson," ESPN, August 4, 2020, https://www.espn.com/nfl/story/_/id /29573631/why-not-late-father-inspires-seahawks-russell-wilson.

father's challenge made Russell think, allowing him the freedom to dream as big as he dared.

And that approach to life continues to drive Russell through his many endeavors. And it's also why he named his foundation "Why Not You," in honor of his father and to encourage children to dream big.

ACHIEVEMENTS

Russell has been a quarterback in the NFL for twelve seasons and now plays for the Denver Broncos after spending ten years with Seattle. During his professional career, he has amassed an outstanding collection of awards and honors and broken many records.

Russell has taken the Seahawks to two consecutive Super Bowls in 2014 and 2015, bringing home the championship title in 2014. The victory made Russell one of three Black quarterbacks to win the Super Bowl.

With 115 wins to date, Russell is one of eighteen players to reach the one hundred mark in NFL history, placing him in an elite category of players.

As a testament to his football mastery, he was chosen for nine Probowls, where the best of the best in the NFL come together to compete. First chosen as a rookie in 2012, he was selected again from 2013 to 2015 and from 2017 to 2021.

Russell is the only quarterback to achieve over forty thousand passing yards to date.

Russell has been recognized for his exemplary work on and off the field throughout his career; in 2012, he received Rookie of the Year; in 2020 and 2021, he received the Walter Payton NFL

Man of the Year Award; and in 2022, he received the Bart Starr Award. Russell is a three-time recipient of one of the Seahawks' most prestigious awards, the Steve Largent Award. A high honor, the Steve Largent Award is "voted on by teammates and given to the player or coach who best exemplifies the spirit, dedication, and integrity of the Seahawks."[40]

LIFE LESSONS

To achieve great things, you first have to believe you can. Russell's father challenged him to believe in himself by asking, "Why not you?" Those three simple words sparked Russell's ambition and his push for excellence in everything he did. It's a good question for anyone looking to follow their dreams to ask themselves. It can help turn negative feelings of doubt and insecurity into hopeful possibilities. Because if not you, then who?

Russell used that principle to guide him through his life, and it helped him become one of the best quarterbacks in the NFL. Though he was discounted because of his height, and some even thought he didn't belong in the NFL at all, he showed how far confidence, hard work, and a positive mindset can take you.

Russell was often asked to prove himself, but he didn't let the doubts of others discourage him. He planned, prepared, and showed up, not just to prove himself but to surpass everyone's expectations. Russell made his childhood dreams come true by showing up for himself.

Imagine what you could do or how far you could go if you just believed you could.

---

40 John Boyle, "Bobby Wagner Named 2023 Steve Largent Award Winner," Seahawks, January 1, 2024, https://www.seahawks.com/news/bobby-wagner -named-2023-steve-largent-award-winner.

FRITZ POLLARD

*"My father had taught me that I was too big
to be humiliated by prejudiced whites."*[41]

EARLY YEARS

Coming in at five feet, nine inches and weighing only 165 pounds, Frederick Douglass Pollard didn't look like your average football player, but what he lacked in size, he made up for in skill, agility, and determination. This small but mighty athlete would become the NFL's first African American player and the first Black coach, blazing a trail for the many who would follow.

Frederick Douglass Pollard, nicknamed "Fritz," was born on January 27, 1894, in the big and bustling city of Chicago, Illinois. Fritz came from a large family where he was the seventh of eight children. He was named after the famous abolitionist Frederick Douglass.

As the only Black family in the wealthy, all-white neighborhood of Rogers Park, the Pollards stood out in the community. They were well-known in the area and, for the most part, accepted. But they did have their fair share of racially motivated conflicts. Still, Fritz's parents believed living in this neighborhood would give their children more opportunities. For them, the benefits outweighed any problems the family encountered. And for Fritz, navigating in this all-white world, where he was undoubtedly a curiosity, helped

---

41 Farrell Evans, "Fritz Pollard Fought for Racial Equality in the NFL," *NBC News*, September 11, 2019, https://www.nbcnews.com/news/nbcblk/fritz-pollard -african-american-founding-father-nfl-n1052046.

prepare him for his years ahead as one of the few Black players in football.

Fritz's father, John William Pollard, was a barber, and his mother, Catherine Amanda Hughes Pollard, was a seamstress. Fritz's parents, both well-educated and successful business owners, believed that a good education was fundamental. They insisted their children perform well academically and attend college. While the Pollard household was happy, Fritz's parents were strict. They placed great importance on achievement, ambition, and being a self-starter.

From an early age, Fritz's father taught the children how to navigate within an all-white world where racism and discrimination were a part of life. And he showed them how to avoid confrontation, if possible, and how to handle it when it occurred. He also taught the boys how to defend themselves when needed. From their mother, the children learned how to be self-starters, set high standards, and believe in themselves. As one of the family's youngest members, Fritz benefitted from the knowledge and experience of his older sisters and brothers, who were eager to teach him what they knew. Fritz found that he would need to lean heavily on the skills and principles his family taught him as he navigated through life.

The emphasis on education in the house ensured Fritz kept up with his studies, even though he didn't enjoy school. He was much more interested in athletics and music. As a boy, Fritz showed a natural talent for sports. He often played in neighborhood baseball and football games. But football was his first love. His older brothers, Leslie and Luther, taught him how to play football and use his size to his advantage. And it helped that he was fast and agile.

Fritz put his natural gifts and learned skills to good use in high school. He attended Lane Technical College Prep High School, where he played on the football, basketball, and track teams. Amazingly, he was a star athlete in all three sports. Always one to keep himself busy, he was also in the school band. But the band was secondary to his athletic pursuits.

In football, Fritz was a great offensive player who was good at running long yards and dodging the opposition. While he enjoyed high school, Fritz had his fair share of encounters with racial discrimination. But he was well liked, and his peers admired his athletic abilities. Though small and slight, he brimmed with confidence and assuredness, contributing to his success on and off the field.

Fritz was named All-County Champion in track and field, for the low hurdles and the half-mile run, and the All-County Shortstop in baseball. In football, he was twice named to the All-County Football League. Clearly, Fritz had the potential to pursue any sport he desired, but he had his mind set on football, his favorite.

When Fritz graduated from high school in 1912, friends and family encouraged him to go to college. He might have been interested in a different path if it were up to him, but he already knew there would be no other option. His parents expected him to further his education. Though he was unsure of where to go for school, one thing Fritz was sure of was his football abilities. He knew he was a gifted player and wanted to prove himself on a platform where he could showcase his talents. He wanted to follow in his older brother Leslie's footsteps and play for a college football team. Leslie, who had attended Dartmouth, had made some leeway in integrating the Dartmouth team, and Fritz thought he might do the same. He knew he was as good or even better than his all-white peers; he just had to get on a team to prove it.

On the advice of friends and family, he set his sights on Northwestern University in Illinois. But he was turned away by the administration. With no backup, Fritz put off his schooling until he could figure out what to do. But what was supposed to be a short delay turned into a long detour.

As he waited, he played football for various semipro teams in the Chicago area. His mother wasn't pleased and wanted Fritz to get back to his college search. She urged him to attend Brown University in Providence, Rhode Island. After some consideration, Fritz found he was as keen as his mother to go to Brown. He started in the spring of 1913 as a "special student," but an administrative issue forced him to leave the school early in his first few weeks.

Fritz was frustrated. He didn't know how he would return home after failing to get into college again. He decided to stay in the city, taking up odd jobs and starting what turned out to be a successful clothes-pressing and tailoring business. One year turned into another before Fritz realized his plans had gotten sidetracked. Somewhere along the way, he had forgotten about his dream of playing college football.

He was embarrassed he still had not entered or completed college. Once again, he turned to friends and family for help. On their advice, he enrolled in one college, and when that didn't work out, he enrolled in another. But Fritz soon found himself bouncing around colleges, looking for a perfect fit to follow his academic and athletic pursuits. He tried Dartmouth, Harvard, and Bates. But he never stayed at any of the colleges for long. There was always one problem or another. Exhausted and deflated by his search, he finally decided to clear up the administrative issue with Brown so he could finally attend the college.

PATH TO SUCCESS

In 1915, Fritz was accepted into Brown. He was happy to finally become part of the student body at the college, and he couldn't wait to join the football team. Three years had passed since he had completed high school, but Fritz wouldn't let the delay stop him from successfully joining the team. He was determined to make up for lost time.

At the Bruins tryouts, he was met with resistance and anger from players on the team who didn't want to have a Black man as a teammate. But Fritz held his head high and did his best to ignore the slurs and snubs. He made an impressive start at tryouts and eventually earned a spot on the team. "His teammates, basically, really wouldn't talk to him or anything until they saw what he could do. Once they saw his talent, he won them over. And his personality also won them over. So from then on, they had his back no matter what,"[42] Fritz Pollard III said of his father's integration of the Brown football team.

Fritz was an exceptional college football player. He knew how to handle the ball and the competition. But he often experienced physical violence from opposing teams and sometimes fans. He was an obvious target for competing teams who underestimated him because he was Black and small. But the more difficult they made it for him, the harder and more skillfully he played. And no one expected that. His bravado and ability to rebound caught his opponents and haters off guard. Even when he found himself at the bottom of a pile-up, where he could easily be attacked, he'd find his way out and continue playing, frustrating the competition.

---

42 Gary Waleik, "Fritz Pollard: The Small Running Back Who Broke Big Barriers | Only a Game," WBUR, January 12, 2018, https://www.wbur.org/onlyagame /2018/01/12/fritz-pollard-football.

With Fritz's place on the team secured, Brown soon became a dominating force on the college football scene, racking up wins, even against first-place teams like Yale University. After their victory against Yale in the fall of 1915, the Black media focused their attention on Fritz. He was already making a mark as a star player. And he attracted large crowds eager to see if a Black man could play football.

While the Brown team couldn't defeat top-ranked Harvard that year, their record earned them an invitation to the 1916 Rose Bowl in Pasadena, California. Fritz was excited, and so were his teammates. The game proved to be a historic occasion on many fronts. Not only was it the first of what would become the annual Rose Bowl Game, but it was Brown's first and only appearance at the Rose Bowl. The occasion also marked the first time an African American would play at the Rose Bowl. On New Year's Day, 1916, The Bruins played against the Washington State Cougars. But the rainy, mud-soaked field would get the best of them. And even Fritz didn't play to his potential. The Bruins lost 14-0, a crushing blow. But the event and Fritz captured the attention of both Black and white fans and the media.

The Bruins' 1916 season was a banner year, with Fritz commanding the field. They beat Yale again and finally had their first-ever win against Harvard. They closed out the season with eight wins and just one loss. Fritz's quick thinking and smart plays during the season earned him a place as the first African American on *The New York Times'* All-American first team and the second African American selected to Walter Camp's All-American halfback team. Pollard felt lucky and ecstatic. The white press ran with the news, bringing national attention to Pollard's work during the season.

"Having been placed on the All-American team by Walter Camp helped me all through my life,"[43] Fritz said years later of the honor that had made him a household name in white and Black America and opened many doors for him.

That year, Fritz continued to excel as an athlete. As his football fame took off, so did his track and field stardom. In the spring of 1916, he broke the world record for low hurdles and qualified for the Olympics, an incredible accomplishment. His celebrity was on the rise, but it came at a cost. His grades suffered. Due to consistently low marks and many absences, he became ineligible to play football and other athletics. Fitz dropped out of college in spring 1918 because of his poor academic standing.

But his love affair with football wasn't over. However, it would take another short detour—one that would eventually lead him back to the game as a professional player.

After leaving college, Fritz was drafted into the Army as physical director at Camp Mead during World War I. And in the fall of 1918, as part of a wartime initiative, he was transferred to Lincoln University, an all-Black College in Oxford, Pennsylvania, to be the head football coach and athletic director.

Fritz was an effective and successful coach at Lincoln. The team went undefeated that season.

He continued to coach at Lincoln in 1919, and his coaching success brought him to the attention of Ralph Waldsmith, the coach and co-owner of the Akron Indian Professionals, a semiprofessional regional team in Ohio. Waldsmith wanted Fritz to play on his team, and Fritz accepted.

---

43 Ronald A. Smith and John M. Carroll, "Fritz Pollard: Pioneer in Racial Advancement," The Journal of American History 79, no. 4 (March 1, 1993): 1655, https://doi.org/10.2307/2080318.

Fritz divided his time and attention in 1919 between his coaching duties at Lincoln University and playing with the Akron team. When he made his first appearance at practice in Akron, none of the other players were happy to see him. But Fritz was there to do a job, so as usual, he set himself to the task, ignoring the rejection. The team had an upcoming game within a few days of Fritz's arrival, and the competition had outwardly threatened violence against him. He was already in the thick of things and had just arrived, but Fritz was used to being targeted and went into the game ready to play. Though the team lost, Fritz once again proved himself on the field. Showcasing his limitless abilities to run, gain yards, and outsmart the competition, he soon became a fan favorite of the Akron fans and a respected player among his teammates. The team finished the season in good standing.

But something was on the horizon for professional football that would change the game. In August 1920, owners from various teams banded together to create a national league, the APFA (the American Professional Football Association), which two years later became the NFL.

Akron was one of the originating members of the new organization. On the heels of the league's formation, they changed their name to the Akron Pros. Fritz made his official professional debut in the NFL with the Akron Pros on October 3, 1920. He was in fine form and contributed greatly to their 43-0 win over the Wheeling Stogies. The team went undefeated that season, outplaying their competition in every game. And much of their success was due to the work of their star player, Fritz Pollard. The Pros won the championship title for their 1920–21 season, topping off a remarkable season.

Fritz's skill on the field singled him out, and he was named to the All-American pro team.

The following year, in 1921, Fritz was hired as head coach of the Akron team while also continuing as a player. The appointment made him the first African American coach in the NFL.

Everything was working in Fritz's favor. But it was all about to change again.

TRIALS AND TRIBULATIONS

With Fritz as head coach of the Akron Pros, everyone had high expectations. But the team floundered that year. Plagued by injuries and changes within the team, the Pros couldn't bring back the magic of the year before. And before the season was up, Fritz was released from his contract. There was no time to wallow, though; he was offered another opportunity as a player-coach in Milwaukee, beginning a pattern that would see him jumping from team to team.

The years after the championship win with the Pros was a hectic time for Fritz, marked by a lot of movement in his professional career. Between 1921 and 1926, he joined the Milwaukee Badgers, the Hammond Pros, the Gilberton Catamounts (a non-NFL team), and the Providence Steamrollers. Fritz played or coached with these teams, often at the same time, juggling duties in different locations and dividing himself in ways that, at times, caused his performance as a player and coach to suffer.

Years of hard playing finally got to Fritz. Repeated injuries and sub-par performances indicated that it was time to call it quits. But before he could retire as he planned, he was released from his contract with the Akron Pros, to which he had returned in early 1926. At thirty-two years old, Fritz played his last NFL game in October 1926.

Through it all, the one thing that was consistent in Fritz's life was the racism he experienced, no matter where he went. As the only Black man in all-white spaces in the racial atmosphere of the time, he was often the target of discrimination and physical violence.

In college, he wasn't allowed to join any fraternities on campus. Nor did any white student want to be his roommate in the dorm. On the football field, opposing teams often didn't want to play with him or roughed him up in an attempt to hurt him. They called him names and made it difficult for him to play. In some games, he had to be escorted onto the field because of the threats against him. At other times, he wasn't allowed to play at all. And he usually wasn't allowed to stay or eat with his teammates or even change in the locker rooms with his teammates.

But Fritz was resilient, and though many wanted to see him suffer in the game, he never gave them the satisfaction. "I'd look at 'em and grin. Didn't get mad and wanna fight 'em. Just look at 'em and grin, and the next minute run 80 yards for a touchdown,"[44] Fritz boasted.

ACHIEVEMENTS

As early as his high school career, Fritz's life had been one of many firsts and accomplishments. Though he is remembered as the first African American to play in the NFL, Fritz was also the first Black football player at Brown University. When the team made it to the Rose Bowl in 1916, he became the first Black man to play in the tournament and the first to be named All-American.

He led the Akron Pros to the championship title in 1920, making him the first African American to play on a championship team.

---

44 Waleik, "Fritz Pollard."

When he joined the Gilberton team, he was the first Black man to play in the coal-mining leagues of Pennsylvania.

Pollard's expertise in the game was admired. Many teams hired him as a player-coach, where he played and helped coach teams to winning games and seasons. Pollard continued to trailblaze as a coach, becoming the first head coach in the NFL in 1923 with his appointment to the Akron Pros. Also, in 1923, he became the first Black quarterback when he played for the Hammond Pros team.

Fritz was one of the most outstanding athletes of his time. His presence on the fields drew crowds in the thousands. And he continued to be a gate attraction until he left the sport in 1926. But even after he retired as a player, he remained invested in the game he loved.

His work promoting football integration defined the decade after Fritz's retirement. Despite the inroads he and others had made in the 1920s and '30s, only a few African American players still played with various teams in the NFL. And by the early '30s, teams had ceased hiring Black players altogether. Fritz was disillusioned and disappointed by this turn of events.

In response to this shutout of Black players in the NFL, Fritz started an all-Black, all-star football team, the Chicago Black Hawks, in 1928. In 1935, he also became head coach of the Brown Bombers, another all-Black professional team in New York. Fritz hired and gave recognition to some of the best African American college and former pro football players in America. He worked hard to continue integration and push for the equality of Black players.

Pollard's accomplishments and dedication to the game resulted in his selection to the College Football Hall of Fame in 1954. He was the first Black player elected.

In 2005, he was inducted into the Professional Football Hall of Fame, nineteen years after he died in 1986. On the momentous occasion of his induction, his grandson Steven Towns gave the enshrinement speech and said, "The seats behind me and in front of me are filled with your legacy. After today everyone will know the gifts you've given to football. From its earliest days from its crowd thrilling game-winning plays to a string of firsts. . . . You've more than earned your place in the history of football."[45]

LIFE LESSONS

Fritz was a superstar in the game of football for good reason. He excelled as both a player and a coach. Known best for his long runs, defensive work, and inventive plays, he helped bring excitement to the games and recognition to the professional league. He was an influential leader capable of inspiring and rallying his teams. Whether people liked him or not, it was hard to dispute his expertise. And thanks to coverage in the Black and white press, his reputation preceded him everywhere he went.

Fritz dared to go beyond the limits of what society told him he could achieve and surpassed everyone's expectations. When others counted him out because of his size or the color of his skin, he used that as fuel to prove everyone wrong.

He didn't allow anyone or anything to stand in the way of his dream. And when presented with an obstacle on and off the field, Fritz found a way around it. He was a man of action, with a strong work ethic and an even stronger belief in himself—qualities necessary for any achiever. And he used those qualities to give him the strength to overcome even the most difficult circumstances.

---

45 "Fritz Pollard's Enshrinement Speech Transcript | Pro Football Hall of Fame," Pro Football Half of Fame, January 1, 2005, https://www.profootballhof.com /news/2005/01/news-fritz-pollard-s-enshrinement-speech-transcript.

As Fritz racked up achievements, he was aware of the doors he was opening for others, and it pleased him to know other Black athletes would have an easier time because of the work he had already put in.

Today, there are many Black players in the NFL, though there are still few coaches. While there is still work to be done, where we are today is owed in many parts to Fritz Pollard's contributions to the game.

CHAPTER 5

GYMNASTICS

SIMONE BILES AND DOMINIQUE DAWES

SIMONE BILES

"No matter if it's inside of sports or outside of sports. It doesn't matter what you look like, where you come from, what religion or ethnicity you are; it's finding that light inside of you and letting it shine."[46]

EARLY YEARS

How do you get to be the world's greatest gymnast? Follow the lead of Simone Biles. Her seven Olympic medals and thirty World Championships put her in a class of her own. But her success isn't just based on how many medals she's won. It's also about how she's navigated her journey to the top. From foster child to gymnastics superstar, Simone has managed the ups and downs of life and her career with integrity. And even as she pursued her dreams, she never lost sight of what was important to her or the love for the sport that brought her so far.

Before the age of six, Simone Arianne Biles's life was pretty tough; she even lived in foster care for a while. Simone was born in Columbus, Ohio, on March 14, 1997, and was the second youngest of her siblings. She lived with her mother, Shanon Biles, her older sister, Ashley, her older brother, Tevin, and her younger sister, Adria. The children were close, but Simone's mom had a hard time caring for her kids because of an addiction to drugs and alcohol. Things started to go badly for the family when Simone was just

---

46 "What More Can I Say? | Simone Biles Is Known as a Four Time Olympic . . . ," Facebook, July 6, 2021, https://www.facebook.com/vsonwatch/videos /234761905126834.

three, and the children were placed in foster care due to neglect. While their foster home was nice, it was only temporary, and the children didn't know what would happen next.

But it was only a matter of time before their grandfather, Ronald Biles, showed up and took the kids into his care. He moved all the kids to Spring, Texas, a Houston suburb, to live with him and his second wife, Nellie, and their sons, Ron II and Adam, who were in high school. It was a happy turn of events, and soon, Simone and her siblings settled into their new surroundings.

But things changed when Simone's mother wanted the children back. Despite feeling crushed, Nellie and Ronald let the children return to Ohio. But Simone's mom was still unable to care for the children, and they all ended up back in foster care. Simone's grandfather was quick to return. He wanted to take the children back to Texas, but Tevin and Ashley wanted to stay in the state close to their mom. A tough decision was made to separate the children, with Tevin and Ashley going to live with a relative in Ohio and Simone and Adria headed back with their grandfather. Nellie and Ronald officially adopted Simone and Adria when Simone was six, and that's how her grandparents became her parents.

Simone was happy at her new home in Texas. Her parents made sure she and her sister had everything they needed to feel loved and cared for.

Simone was very close to her sister. They spent most of their time together and with neighborhood friends. Growing up, some of their favorite pastimes included jumping rope, riding their bikes, and playing soccer. Simone was an energetic, fun-loving, imaginative, and adventurous girl who had a fondness for turtles, one of her favorite animals to this day.

Simone's other favorite activity was the trampoline at the back of the house. She spent many days with her siblings in the backyard, soaring, jumping, trying new tricks, and enjoying every moment.

One day, a random daycare field trip would change what she did in her spare time into her greatest passion. Simone was just six years old when the daycare she and Adria attended took a field trip to Bannon's Gymnastix, a tumbling gym nearby. As soon as Simone entered the gym, she knew this was just the place for her. She tried out the equipment; she tumbled, jumped, flipped, and leaped to her heart's content. And she was good at it. There and then, she fell in love with gymnastics.

Showing off her moves got her noticed by one of the staff at the gym, who gave Simone a personal invitation to enroll. She was excited to return, and her parents thought it would be a good activity for the girls, so they signed them up. Simone was ecstatic.

She started attending classes weekly. Aimee Boorman, her coach for eleven years, knew there was something special about Simone when she first saw her at Bannon's. She was surprised that Simone could copy and execute complex skills effortlessly, and her upper body strength and petite physique were perfect for gymnastics. Simone quickly excelled, performing more challenging moves as she progressed. Aimee knew Simone had the potential to go far in gymnastics if she wanted to. And Simone wanted that more than anything.

Soon, Simone had dreams of making the US Junior National Gymnastics team. She worked hard, practicing her skills and putting in plenty of training time. The 2011 Visa National Championships in Saint Paul, Minnesota, was around the corner. It would be her debut as an elite gymnast, but more importantly, how well she did at this meet would determine whether she was selected to join the junior team. Her performances earlier that year gave her good reason to be hopeful. She had placed third in the all-around competition and first in the vault at the 2010 American Classic Junior national competition in Houston. But was she good enough?

At the trials in Saint Paul, Simone's dreams came crashing down. Her performance placed her in fourteenth place, but there were only thirteen spots on the team. She felt disappointed after all her training and hard work. Narrowly missing the spot broke her heart. It was one of her lowest points, but her mom was there to help put it all into perspective. "You don't go out there to beat another person. You go out there to do your very best. If your very best means you win the competition, that's the way it should be. If your very best means you come in 3rd or 4th, that's fine too. As long as you did your best."[47] Her mom's good advice comforted Simone. Whenever the pressure was too great, or she doubted herself, she would remember it.

While she could have given up on her dream then, she used the disappointment as fuel to push her even harder toward her goal. Simone knew if she wanted to secure a spot the next time, she had to work on the areas where she was weaker. She focused on her execution, precision, difficulty of skills, and conquering the events she found most challenging.

At fourteen years old, Simone was just four feet, eight inches. She was muscular, strong, and determined. She knew if she set her mind to it, she could conquer whatever obstacle was in her way. But it would take more than physical ability to get her to where she wanted to be. She had to put in more time. That meant changing her schedule to allow for more training time. But that also meant Simone had to change schools, leaving her friends.

47 Simone Biles, *Courage to Soar: A Body in Motion, a Life in Balance*, (Grand Rapids, MI: Zondervan, 2018).

Her parents moved her to a school close to the gym, where she could finish grades seven and eight. With the extra time, Simone brought her training up to twenty to thirty hours a week.

By the time 2012 arrived, Simone felt better than ever. She had put the work in, and it showed. That year, she earned first place in the all-around competition at the US and American Classic Tournaments. She had mastered more complex moves and performed with such ease and agility that she impressed everyone watching. She waited anxiously to see if she would make the team. And guess what? She had improved so much that she came in third in the all-around event, earning a spot on the US National team. She had done it! She was finally on her way, and there would be no looking back.

Simone fantasized about going to the London Olympics in 2012, just a few months away, but at fifteen, she was underage. That dream would have to wait. In the meantime, she would continue to compete in other competitions, honing her skills. She knew that many gymnasts often reached their peak in high school, but she was hopeful that wouldn't be her. The Olympics was a far-off dream; after all, they were another four years away. Her more immediate dream was to attend a top college and compete at the collegiate gymnastics level after high school.

As for high school, Simone decided to be home-schooled for grades nine through twelve. Though she had always wanted to attend high school with her friends, it was impossible now that she was training at an elite level. So Simone was forced to sacrifice one dream for another.

PATH TO SUCCESS

In 2013, things started to take off for Simone. She dazzled at the P&G National, becoming the all-around national champion that year. She was then named to the senior team and selected for her first World Championships.

It was Simone's first international trip with the team, and it was a surreal experience. She made an impressive first appearance, capturing first place in the all-around and the floor, making her the first Black woman to win the event at Worlds. She also won silver for vault and bronze for beam.

But her novice appearance at Worlds was also remarkable for another reason. It was the first time she performed and perfectly executed a floor skill of her own creation—a double back layout with a half twist. As is customary in gymnastics, when a gymnast performs a new move at an international event, the move is thereafter known by the gymnast's name. Hence, the first gymnastic move named "Biles" was born. But there would be others.

Simone started 2014 with an injured shoulder, which made her sit out of some competitions, but she finished the year strong. In August, she returned to competition in fine form for the National Championships in Pittsburgh, Pennsylvania. There, she defended the all-around champion title and won first place a second time. She also won gold on the vault and floor and tied for silver on the beam. Once again, she was selected for the national team and chosen to attend the World Championships.

For a second time at Worlds, Simone won the all-around title. She also won three other golds during the event: two for her performances on beam and floor and the team event. Her final award was a silver medal for vault.

Simone continued to wow in 2015. At the US Classic, she won the all-around, beam, vault, and floor exercises. Then, at the Nationals, she won the all-around championship for a third time. The World Championships were on the horizon, and Simone was feeling pressure to perform as well as she had done before. Many people believed she would, but their expectations only added to her worry. She didn't want to let anyone down.

Despite her fears, Simone gave an outstanding performance at the World Championships in Glasgow, Scotland. She won the all-around championship and gold medals for her work on the beam and the floor. She made history again, becoming the first woman to win three consecutive World Championships. With fourteen total medals from her three appearances, ten of them gold, she was now the most decorated American female gymnast in the event's history. She was named Team USA Athlete of the Year for her stellar year.

Her win at the Worlds was the beginning of Simone's rise to superstardom. The fans and the media couldn't get enough of the petite gymnast with the charming personality and big smile. It seemed everyone was paying attention to the young gymnast and three-time Worlds champion. Sponsorship offers began pouring in. But Simone had a tough decision ahead of her—what to do about school. The time had finally come to decide on a college. And, of course, she was a much sought-after prospect. Many colleges vied for her attention, but she had her heart set on UCLA. She looked forward to college life and all that came with it.

But what seemed so sure before now was not. With sponsorship offers pouring in, Simone faced another dilemma. Attend college or turn pro? After much family discussion and contemplation, she opted to turn pro and defer college.

With her decision made and the Worlds behind her, she turned her attention to the Olympics. She was the favorite to make the US Olympic team, another dream she intended to follow, but she didn't want to get ahead of herself. She trained hard with the hope of making the team but continued to take the path one step at a time, aiming to do her very best at every competition along the way.

As it turned out, Simone had nothing to worry about. At the Olympic trials in San Jose, California, she placed first. She had made it to the Olympic team, and one of her biggest dreams had come true. Now, she would be sharing the limelight with Olympic champions Gabby Douglas, Aly Reisman, and other top gymnasts Laurie Hernandez and Madison Kocian on the team. She was excited to start her Olympic adventure.

The whole experience was everything Simone had dreamt of and more. The Olympic Village was a wonderland where she met world-famous athletes, participated in Olympic ceremonies, and bonded with her teammates. However, the time moved quickly as the team trained rigorously for the upcoming events.

Again, all eyes were on Simone. Expectations were high that she would bring home multiple medals. But she wasn't sure she could live up to everyone's hopes.

The team performed flawlessly and won team gold for the US. That day, they made history as the most decorated American gymnastics team. In addition to the team medal, Simone took home gold in the all-around, vault, and floor exercises. She also won bronze on the beam.

As she stood on the podium, with the audience cheering wildly, Simone was so happy and proud. She had really done it!

She was nineteen, at the top of her game, and not yet ready to hang up her leotard. But she did want to attend college, as planned. But a traditional school obviously wouldn't work with her schedule. So, she said another goodbye to her UCLA aspirations to continue pursuing her athletic one. She chose an online school, University of the People, where she majored in business administration.

After a brief break, Simone returned to competition in 2018. She swept all five events at the National Championships, winning gold in all-around, beam, vault, floor, and uneven bars. At the World Championships that year, she kept the streak going. She won four gold medals, a silver, and a bronze. Her medal collection made her the most decorated female gymnast in world history. And she wasn't finished yet.

Simone became a six-time champion at the National Championships in 2019, when she won the all-around title yet again. And her return to the World Championships, held that year in Stuttgart, Germany, would bring another round of medals. Simone won gold in the team, balance beam, floor, and vault. She also won gold in the all-around, making it her fifth time and making her the first woman to reach that marker. With her medal sweep, she became the most medalled gymnast, male or female, at the Worlds.

TRIALS AND TRIBULATIONS

But Simone would face some of her biggest hardships in the years following her first Olympic win. And these challenges would test her as an athlete and as a person.

In 2015 it was discovered that Larry Nassar, a Team USA Gymnastics doctor, sexually abused many of the girls and women under his care. As investigations were launched into the accusations, many of Simone's teammates and friends came forward to say they were some of his victims. In January 2018, Simone also came forward to say the doctor had abused her. It was something she still hadn't come to terms with, and it was painful for her to relive the experiences she and others had with Nassar. Simone fell into a depression. But she knew by using her voice and platform, she could call attention to the matter and help bring awareness of sexual abuse. She hoped other girls and women wouldn't experience what she and the other victims had been through. It was a difficult time for Simone and her teammates, who leaned on each other for support. Nassar was found guilty of the charges against him and ultimately sentenced to prison. Because of Simone's actions, the training center where Nassar perpetrated his assaults was shut down.

In September 2021, Simone and other renowned athletes, Aly Reisman, Maggie Nichols, and McKayla Maroney, testified in front of the Senate about their experiences with Nassar. Though she blamed the system for keeping Nassar's abuse secret, which allowed the abuse to go on for many years, she also had a more profound outlook on the experience, saying, "I couldn't punish myself or blame it on gymnastics because it wasn't gymnastics fault, and I couldn't let it take away my happiness or my comeback or what I was doing or what my goals were for when I came back to the sport. Some of those things that shaped you into who you were, you can't change. And that's the reason why you are the way you are. You can't erase them so you have to embrace them."[48]

After such a grueling experience, Simone refused to be defined by it or let it tarnish all she had achieved or was yet to achieve. She set her mind toward her next goal, the upcoming Olympics in Tokyo, Japan. But that, too, would test her in ways she hadn't been tested before.

---

48 "What More Can I Say?," Facebook.

The 2020 Olympics in Tokyo, Japan, were rescheduled to the summer of 2021 due to COVID. It was supposed to be a great comeback for Simone, who had spent the last couple of years intensively training for the event. But something happened that she couldn't have predicted. It forced her to do something she had never done before—withdraw from the events in which she was scheduled to participate.

While performing her vault routine, the first event in the team final, Simone lost track of where she was in the air. Known as the "twisties" in gymnastics circles, it is incredibly disorienting and dangerous for gymnasts.

Simone rallied and managed to complete her performance without using any twists. But it was just the beginning of a disappointing turn of events. She withdrew from each event she was to appear in as she struggled to manage the twisties. Everyone was shocked, and the press pushed for answers. She explained she would be taking time off to prioritize her mental health. Her decision met a surprising amount of backlash from critics and fans alike, who felt she had let the team down. But Simone stayed focused on getting better, knowing she had made the right decision for herself and her teammates. She returned to compete in the balance beam, her last event, on the final day of the competition. She took the twists out of her routine, knowing she would lose points on difficulty. Despite the changes, she still completed a polished and effortless routine, earning a bronze for her performance.

Simone was disappointed and hurt not only by her inability to compete in the games the way she had envisioned but also by the negative response to her mental health break. Nevertheless knowing she had struggled through the twisties and still performed on the last day filled her with pride. Simone's experience brought attention and much-needed discussion on the topic of mental health in sports. "It's something that people go through a lot that's kind of pushed under the rug. I feel like we're not just entertainment, we're humans as well. We have feelings. And at the end of the day, people don't understand what we're going through."[49]

ACHIEVEMENTS

Simone Biles is one of the world's most recognized athletes, and with good reason. Over the past ten-plus years of her career, she has collected various awards and medals, making her the most decorated gymnast in history.

From her earliest debut as an elite gymnast in 2013, when she blasted onto the national and international stage, Simone has continued to set standards and break records.

She has a whopping thirty-seven World Championship titles, twenty-three of which are gold. Simone earned her last championship wins at the 2023 Worlds in Antwerp, Belgium, where she picked up another three gold medals in the all-around, beam, and floor and a bronze on the uneven bars.

She has participated in six World Championships and been crowned the all-around winner in all of them, setting a new record. And she has the most medals of any gymnast in World Championship history.

---

49 Jason Aten, "Simone Biles's 12-Word Response to the Possibility of Not Making the Olympics Is One of the Best Examples of Emotional Intelligence I've Seen," *Inc.*, January 29, 2024, https://www.inc.com/jason-aten/simone-biles-12-word -response-to-not-making-olympics-is-best-example-of-emotional-intelligence -ive-seen-yet.html.

Simone is a two-time Olympic medalist, competing in the 2016 Olympics in Rio de Janeiro, Brazil, and the 2020 Olympics in Tokyo, Japan. She has seven Olympic medals, four of which are gold.

She also has developed five skills that were added to the Artistic Gymnastics Code of Points, all with a high degree of difficulty. The first skill, a floor move, she debuted in 2013, called the Biles, is a double back layout with a half twist. The Biles was followed by the Biles II in 2019, another floor move characterized by two flips and three twists in a tucked position. Also, 2019 saw the unveiling of her first balance beam dismount, the Biles, a double-twisting backflip. And her final two moves are on the vault. The Biles I, unveiled in 2021, is a roundoff, back handspring with half-turn entry. The Biles II, performed in 2023, is a roundoff, back handspring with a double flip in the piked position.

In 2022, the President awarded Simone with the highest honor a nonmilitary person can receive in the US. For her advocacy work with mental health, adoption, and sexual abuse, she received the Presidential Medal of Freedom.

LIFE LESSONS

In the physically demanding sport of gymnastics, Simone has mastered skills like no other, pushing herself beyond expectation and reaching unimaginable heights.

Along the way to becoming the most decorated gymnast, she found herself and realized her love for the sport propelled her forward. She realized early on she was blessed with an ability, and it was her calling to pursue it. She never lost sight of her goals, herself, or how happy the sport made her.

Simone lived her life following her mom's advice. She showed up to every event intent on doing her best while leaving others' expectations behind.

While she gave up many things to become who she is today, it was all worth it in her eyes. A chance to follow her dreams, surpass them, and lead a life beyond her wildest imagination is the ultimate fulfillment.

Simone has shown that following your heart, bouncing back from setbacks, and doing your very best go hand in hand with determination, hard work, and perseverance.

As a role model, Simone takes her responsibility seriously and knows that the children who look up to her keenly observe every step she takes. Conscious of her impact, she stated, "I wanted every child, regardless of race to be able to look at my Worlds win and say I can dream big too. I wanted them to know that following your dreams, not just in gymnastics but in everything, shouldn't have anything to do with the color of your skin. It should only be about finding the discipline and the courage to do the hard work."[50]

Simone is still following her dreams, looking ahead to the 2024 Olympics. Who knows what unimaginable feats she'll accomplish there? But one thing is for sure: she'll do it on her own terms and all for the love of the sport.

---

50 Biles, *Courage to Soar.*

DOMINIQUE DAWES

"Make sure you're doing things for the right reason; also, you have to have a passion for what you're doing. I always tell people to follow your heart, but also to be very selective in the people you choose to get advice from and to surround yourself with."[51]

Did you know the first Black woman of any nationality to win an individual Olympic medal in gymnastics was an American named Dominique Dawes? And would you be surprised to find out she was just six years old when she fell in love with the sport? Her love turned into a passion, and her passion turned into a journey of a lifetime. Dominique would accomplish unimaginable feats in gymnastics, paving the way for many aspiring gymnasts to follow in her path.

EARLY YEARS

Dominique Margaux Dawes was born on November 20, 1976, to Don and Loretta Dawes. She grew up in a tight-knit community in Takoma Park, close to Silver Spring, Maryland, and the nation's capital, DC. Dominique is the middle child of the family. She has a sister, Daniella, who is four years older than she is, and a brother, Don Jr., who is six years younger.

---

51 "Dominique Dawes' Hair Story—'I Am Finally Natural!'" Curly Nikki, September 10, 2021, https://www.curlynikki.com/2012/08/dominique-dawes-hair-story-i-am -finally.html.

Growing up, Dominique played with her siblings and her close cousins. Church was also a big part of the Dawes household. Her parents were Baptists, and attending church was a regular family activity. Faith was always important to Dominique growing up and was the foundation she leaned on throughout her life, in the good times and bad.

Even as a toddler, Dominique was an active little girl who kept her parents on their toes. She liked to tumble around the house, flip herself over furniture, and slide down staircases. With such an energetic child, her parents were eager to find outlets to keep her busy. They enrolled her in a few activities, such as ballet and tap lessons, but nothing clicked. That is until the day she walked into a gymnastics gym in Wheaton, Maryland.

Dominique was just six when her mother brought her and her sister to Hills Angels Gymnastics Club. And what she saw there excited her in a way nothing else had. She watched as children jumped, backflipped, rolled, and somersaulted all around her, and that's when she "immediately fell in love. I saw what the big kids were doing and I was like I'm going to do that someday."[52]

At the young age of six, she couldn't have predicted how right she would be nor how big of an impact gymnastics would have on her life. Her mother enrolled Dominique and her sister in the gym, happy to find a place to keep her girls busy.

Kelli Hill, a young former gymnast fresh out of college, ran the gym. Hill was interested in Dominique from the start. She could tell there was something special about the little girl and could see

52 Cale Clarke—The Faith Explained Institute, "My Conversation with Olympic Gold Medalist Dominique Dawes," YouTube, July 23, 2021, https://www.youtube .com/watch?v=hkxfCDKevvY.

she was "very strong. Powerful. Willing to try anything."[53] Those attributes, combined with Dominique's natural abilities and general enthusiasm for the sport, made Hill believe Dominique had potential. Hill would end up coaching Dominique her entire career.

At first, Dominique, like most kids her age, enjoyed the playful aspect of the sport. It was fun to tumble, jump, and somersault. And trying to conquer new equipment like the balance beam and vault was exciting. Though she had her first competition when she was nine and became a junior elite gymnast by age ten, it wasn't until she was eleven that she started to take the sport seriously.

But Dominique didn't just skyrocket to fame; she had to work her way there. It would take years of training and competing before her performances were good enough to earn top grades from the judges. Her motto, "Determination, Dedication, Desire," or D3 as she referred to it, helped her build the mental mindset she needed to persevere.

Dominique made the National Women's team when she was eleven years old. At her first US Championship meet in 1988, she came in seventeenth place. While an honorable placement, Dominique was disappointed she didn't do better. She felt sure she could. And she would have other opportunities along the way to prove it. At twelve years old, in 1989, she attended her first international meet at the Konica Gymnastics Grand Prix in Brisbane, Australia. She placed sixteenth in the all-around event. Nevertheless, it was a thrilling adventure for young Dominique, who was honored to represent her country. But proving that even athletes

---

53 Bill Glauber, "Vaulting onto the Olympics Stage; Marylander's Career Began at McDonald's," *Baltimore Sun*, October 25, 2018, https://www.baltimoresun.com /1992/05/31/vaulting-onto-the-olympic-stage-marylanders-career-began-at -mcdonalds.

have bad days, she remembers falling on her best event at the end of the meet and landing on her head.

When the Nationals came around again in 1990, she was more skilled and experienced. Dominique earned third place in the all-around event. She showed immense growth as a gymnast in just a short matter of time.

Dominique had big dreams. She would write about her aspirations in her journal, chronicling her intention to compete in the 1992 and 1996 Olympics. And she was determined to make those dreams come true.

As a gymnast, Dominique's acrobatic skills were impressive. She was a dynamo on floor exercises, moving with energy and excitement and astounding viewers with her high-flying aerial moves. She quickly became known for her dynamic back-to-back tumbling techniques. She maneuvered through each event with style and grace and always had a smile for the audience and judges. Her small but muscular frame appeared to handle each challenge with ease.

As she got older and competed in more competitions, her training intensified. Similar to having a job, Dominique would clock thirty to forty hours of training every week. It was common for her to spend hours every day at the gym. A typical day included waking up early and training for a couple of hours before school, then training for another three or four hours after school. The sport consumed her life, leaving little time between practice and frequent competitions.

But she was working toward a greater goal, and she was closer than ever to getting there. In 1991, Dominique placed first in her floor routine at the US Gymnastics Championships in Cincinnati, Ohio—a win that proved she was making impressive progress.

In 1992, Dominique emerged from the shadows and into the limelight of public attention. All her hard work paid off that year, culminating in important milestones for the young gymnast. She took first place on the uneven bars at the US Gymnastics Championships. She placed fourth at the US Olympic trials, securing a spot on the US Olympic team, making her the first Black woman to achieve this distinction. The US team won the bronze medal at the Olympic games in Barcelona, Spain. The win was another first for Dominique, who became the first Black woman to win an Olympic medal in gymnastics. The year continued on a high note with her win at the Dodge Gymnastics Challenge: USA vs. Japan, where she came first in the all-around and received a rare perfect score of ten for her work on the floor as part of the team event.

In 1993, she continued to dominate at national and international meets. Some of her most significant achievements that year included winning two silver medals at the World Championships in Birmingham, Great Britain, gold in the US Classic in the all-around event, and gold at the National Championships for her performance on the vault.

As Dominique's star was rising in gymnastics, she was still an average teenager at home, and she still had to go to school. She started off her high school years at Montgomery Blair High School in Silver Spring, Maryland. But, when she was fourteen, she and her family made the difficult decision for her to move in with her coach. Hill had moved her gym to a large facility in Gaithersburg. However, the further distance meant a much longer commute for Dominique and her parents. Paired with her already packed schedule, driving the extra time wouldn't work if she wanted to pursue gymnastics at an elite level. The family decided the move was best. But Dominique visited with her family on weekends or when her schedule allowed.

Hill had two young boys, and Dominique fell in line as just another family member. Hill assumed somewhat of a guiding role. She instilled in Dominique a strong work ethic, a desire to reach her full potential, and an emphasis on education.

Dominique transferred to Gaithersburg High School, where she would finish off her high school education. Despite her grueling practice schedule, she maintained good grades throughout school, graduating on the honor roll. Though Dominique missed out on many social activities throughout the school year, she attended her prom after some coaxing from Hill, where she was crowned prom queen.

In 1994, the year that Dominique graduated, she received a full scholarship from Stanford University. But she wasn't quite ready to start. She felt like she still had unfinished business. She had been so young at her first Olympics and felt sure she could do more if she could participate in the upcoming 1996 games as a more seasoned gymnast. With this goal in mind, Dominique deferred schooling, opting to continue her athletic pursuits. When she made it to the Olympics in 1992, Dominique was just fifteen. She had already realized her childhood Olympic dreams, but at seventeen, she knew much more was left in her.

PATH TO SUCCESS

On August 27, 1994, Dominique showed the country her full potential. At the National Championships in Nashville, Tennessee, she stole the show. Her outstanding performances on the balance beam, vault, uneven bars, and floor competitions earned her first place in each event. She also secured the win in the all-around competition. What an incredible achievement. It had been twenty-five years since any other gymnast swept the competition in all events. It was a historic and unforgettable night for seventeen-year-old Dominique, and it would stoke her desire to compete in the upcoming Olympics.

When asked what motivated her, she cited the "road to Atlanta. I really want to make it there. I really want to help out the US team."[54] The 1996 Olympics were just around the corner, and Dominique had her heart set on being a part of the team.

While Dominique was beloved by the media and fans alike—she was commonly referred to as "Awesome Dawson," a nickname coined by her teammates—it didn't stop her from receiving criticism for her decision to participate in the 1996 Olympics. It's hard to believe, but at nineteen years old, Dominique was considered old for gymnastics. Typically, sixteen is considered a gymnast's prime years, and Dominique was well past that age. Many wondered if she could pull it off.

But when 1996 rolled around, Dominique proved she was still a force to be reckoned with. At the Olympic trials held in Boston, Massachusetts, she came in first in the all-around event, earning a spot on the Olympic team. It was an incredible team comprised of championship winners like Dominique Moceanu, Shannon Miller, and other elite gymnasts in the country. Dominique was in good company. And many believed the team was destined for greatness.

The Atlanta Olympics would see Dominique at one of her lowest and highest points. She faltered before walking into the Georgia Dome, packed with over forty thousand spectators. The pressure of the games, the weight of the competition, and the importance of her role were suddenly overwhelming. She broke down in tears,

---

54 Dailymotion, "Dominique Dawes Interview—1995 US Gymnastics Championships, Women, Event Finals," last accessed June 18, 2024, https://www.dailymotion.com/video/x655dtd.

unable to go any further. But her teammate came out to help her, and together they prayed. Dominique knew she wasn't alone and could depend on her teammates, giving her the strength to carry on.

The team outperformed the competition and took home the gold medal. They were the first US Olympic women's gymnastics team to win gold at the Olympics. The powerhouse team rightfully became known as the "Magnificent Seven." As part of the team, Dominique became the first Black woman to win a gold medal in gymnastics.

Dominique also won bronze in her event, making her the first African American woman to win an individual medal in artistic gymnastics.

"It was so large," Dawes said of her Olympic experience. "There were so many people in the stands cheering. It was kind of scary, but also exciting."[55]

With another Olympic win behind her, Dominique decided it was time to retire from gymnastics. She wanted to complete her college education and see what else life had to offer. But as always, Dominique kept herself busy. She attended the University of Maryland while pursuing acting and modeling opportunities. She even performed on Broadway.

Though she tried to move past gymnastics, leaving it all behind wasn't easy. The fans wanted her to come back. They inundated her with messages and fan mail, and she wanted to come back too, saying at the time, "I really feel that I have it in me, that I can

---

55 Jennifer Frey, "Not Too Old for Games," *Washington Post*, June 25, 1996, https://www.washingtonpost.com/wp-srv/sports/olympics/daily/june/28/notold .htm.

do the sport and do it well. The love and desire for the sport is what drew me back."[56]

Dominique began training for the Olympics in April, just four months ahead of the games. It was a tense time, and though she had come home a winner from the other Olympic games, there were no guarantees she would automatically make this team. She had to try out like everyone else. At the trials, Dominique came in seventh in the all-around, enough to earn her a spot on the Olympic team.

The 2000 Olympic Games, held in Sydney, Australia, would be Dominique's last Olympics. She was eager to end her career on a high note. While her individual performances were lacking, she performed well in the team events. But she and her teammates were edged out by China, who won the bronze medal. But in a twist of fate, ten years later, it was discovered that one of the Chinese gymnasts in the competition was underage, a violation of Olympic gymnastic rules. China was disqualified and stripped of their medal. The US team was then awarded the third-place win.

That turn of events would put Dawes in another rare category: as only one of three people to win medals at three different Olympic games and be a member of three medal-winning teams.

TRIALS AND TRIBULATIONS

Dominique officially retired from gymnastics in 2000, soon after the Olympics. At twenty-three years old, she still had a lifetime of living ahead of her. But what she achieved in two decades as an elite gymnast is nothing short of amazing.

---

56 Staff, "Dawes Hoping for Spot on 2000 Olympic Team," *Buffalo News*, May 24, 2000, https://buffalonews.com/news/dawes-hoping-for-spot-on-2000 -olympic-team/article_d578f00e-c4f9-536c-8198-dfbdaf12c3cd.html

Her life is an inspiring one of self-motivation, knowing what you want, and being determined to pursue it. But it came at a grave cost.

While a young Dominique was hyper-focused on following her dreams, she sacrificed much of her childhood to get there. At the time, it didn't seem to faze her. "The only childhood memory I can remember was spent in a gym. . . . But this is what I enjoy, so it's never bothered me that I was spending all my time in a gym instead of a playground. I'm proud of the things I've accomplished,"[57] a seventeen-year-old Dawes once said in an interview.

But her lost childhood is something an older Dominique looks back on with regret. "I went through a very challenging childhood, in some degree, where I sacrificed my childhood to win an Olympic gold medal."[58]

After she left the sport, her relationship with her coach, Hill, was fractured. Dominique spoke out about the atmosphere at Hill's gym, sharing that it wasn't positive or healthy. The toxic environment led to a lot of anxiety and self-doubt. But Dominique still has faith in gymnastics and sports in general because she believes there is so much children can learn from sports, including a "healthy level of commitment, hard work, perseverance, leaning on teammates. That's what I love about athletics. . . . Sports does prepare young people for many parts of the journey in life: hard work, goal setting, team work, persevering, getting back up after

57 Mike Preston, "Dawes' Golden Life Has Few Free Moments Gymnastics," *Baltimore Sun*, October 24, 2018, https://www.baltimoresun.com/1994/10/15/dawes-golden-life-has-few-free-moments-gymnastics.

58 Natalie Rose Goldberg, "Four-Time Olympic Medalist Dominique Dawes on How She Defines Success," CNBC, August 3, 2023, https://www.cnbc.com/2023/08/03/four-time-olympic-medalist-dominique-dawes-on-how-she-defines-success.html.

you've fallen . . . I learned so much from the most painful moments in my life than I did the victories."[59]

To help foster positive interactions with gymnastics, Dominique started her own gym, the Dominique Dawes Gymnastics Academy, where children can learn about the sport in an empowering and healthy way. At the gym, emphasis isn't placed on whether a child has the potential to be an elite gymnast or win gold medals; rather, it's about encouragement, enjoyment, and healthy development of the whole child within the sport.

Dominique also faced challenges because of her race. In the predominantly white-dominated sport of gymnastics, there was no other Black gymnast for her to look up to or emulate. No one looked like her, a fact Dominique was painfully aware of. And it was difficult at times to know that she would often be the only person of color at a competition. But she shouldered the responsibility with pride, knowing what it would mean to little Black girls and boys to see her on a world stage doing extraordinary things. She became the role model that she so desperately needed.

But one day at the 1996 Olympics, she met Dianne Durham, the first Black woman to win the US Gymnastics National Championship in 1983. Dominique didn't know much of Durham's story, but she later discovered more and was honored that Dianne not only took the time to meet her but also give her a special gift, a box of daily affirmation cards for Dominique to use while at the Olympics. Dianne Durham, like Dominique, faced discrimination in the field and rose above it. And in her story, Dominique found solidarity.

As one of a few Black women in the sport who performed within elite circles, Dominique faced a lot of scrutiny because of her

---

59 Cale Clarke, "My Conversation with Olympic Gold Medalist Dominique Dawes," YouTube, 2021.

race, especially from the event judges. In a time when European features and physiques were favored, Dominique didn't fit in. She was deducted points regularly for essentially being who she was. Every time she walked into an event, she knew she would be judged for everything from her hair to her flat feet, curved back, and skin color. She could do nothing about it except outperform her competition, and that's exactly what she did. Dominique had to work twice as hard to overcome the systemic discrimination within the sport and prove she was as good as any other gymnast on the mats.

ACHIEVEMENTS

Dominique Dawes has so much to be proud of on and off the mat. From her first competition to her last, she took the gymnastics world by storm. Her natural ability, on-stage charisma, steely determination, and one-of-a-kind performances made her a top athlete in a sport in which only the best of the best can compete. Dominique has received countless awards, medals, and championship titles and earned her way to the top with sweat, tears, and hard work.

Some of the most outstanding moments in her career began when she was fifteen years old in 1991. It was the first time she made the National Championships, and she didn't disappoint, coming in first place for her floor routine. It was her first step toward many more memorable performances. She really started to shine in 1992. Dominique made the World Championships team and went on to win the uneven bars event in the competition. But the highlight of that year was the Olympics, where she and her teammates won bronze for their work in the team final. This win made Dominique the first Black gymnast to receive an Olympic medal for gymnastics.

But it was her achievements in 1994 that set her apart from others. At the National Championships, she dominated the meet, sweeping all four categories: vault, uneven bars, balance beam, and floor exercise, as well as the all-around event.

In 1996, Dominique and her teammates won the gold medal in the team event at the Olympics. And at those Olympics, Dominique became the first Black woman of any nationality to win an Olympic gold medal. She also won a bronze medal for her floor exercise routine, making her the first Black woman to win an individual award for gymnastics at the Olympics.

Dominique retired after the 1996 Olympics, but not for long. She returned for the 2000 games in Sydney, Australia, where she and her teammates won bronze.

In total, Dominique won fifteen US Championships and four Olympic medals, including an individual bronze and three team medals (a gold in 1996 and a bronze in 1992 and 2000).

For her achievements, Dawes has received numerous awards and honors. Her recent induction into the Maryland State Athletic Hall of Fame in 2023 makes her the first gymnast to be honored there. Dominique was also inducted into the US Gymnastics Hall of Fame in 2005, the International Gymnastics Hall of Fame in 2009, and the US Olympics Hall of Fame in 2009.

LIFE LESSONS

Any young achiever should possess self-motivation, determination, a strong work ethic, and ceaseless drive. As a three-time Olympian, we know Dominique possessed those qualities in abundance. She dedicated many years to becoming one of the best at her sport, earning her spot on every Olympic and national team. Yet, she never took anything for granted, putting in hours of training and competition.

But some of the biggest takeaways from Dominique's story can be found in what she had to say years after her dynamic rise to the top: "Listen to your heart, listen to your conscience. Don't feel the need to have accolades from the outside world,"[60] says Dominique. Her inspiring story reminds us that true fulfillment comes from following your heart, not fame. So whether your dream is big or small, if it means something to you, it's worth pursuing, and more importantly, you should love what you do.

Looking back, Dominique credits gymnastics for making her who she is but also cautions us not to get lost in ambition or to sacrifice everything. What's important is personal well-being and having positive people and support systems to help you follow your dream.

"I embraced the fact that what I was doing was inspiring and empowering people. . . . I recognized the importance of what I was doing and that I could change someone's life. . . . Young girls and boys would write me. And that's what motivated me to endure what I was enduring for so many years. So when I marched out in the 1992 games in Barcelona, I knew there was going to be a young African American girl or a young girl of color who's going to say, 'Hey, I want to do what this girl is doing.' And the fact that I could plant that seed and inspire a generation was truly a blessing."[61]

Dominique saw her sacrifice as part of a larger calling. She carried the hopes of many Black people, old and young, with her, and she didn't let them down.

---

60 Dana Carter, "Dominique Dawes, Hello My Name Is Dana Podcast Interview," YouTube, August 5, 2022, https://www.youtube.com/watch?v=jhnhhDkskE8.
61 Cale Clarke, "My Conversation with Olympic Gold Medalist Dominique Dawes."

CHAPTER 6

TRACK
AND FIELD

ALLYSON FELIX
AND ALICE COACHMAN

ALLYSON FELIX

*"I think we all should be wildly ambitious
and go after our greatest dreams."*[62]

EARLY YEARS

You don't get to be the most decorated Olympian in track and field history by chance. Just ask Allyson Felix. With thirty-one career medals, including eleven Olympic medals, she is a track and field icon. Allyson knows following your dreams requires dedication, determination, and a willingness to learn from failure. And what her inspirational story can teach us is what the best athletes already know: success isn't about the destination; it's about the journey.

Allyson Felix was born in Los Angeles, California, in 1985. She is the youngest child of Paul Felix and Marlene Felix and has an older brother, Wes. Allyson grew up in a loving home centered on faith and God. Her father, a pastor and seminary professor, and her mother, a teacher, emphasized believing in yourself, working hard, and doing for others. Those principles shaped Allyson into the person she would become and helped her reach the pinnacle of her track and field career.

Allyson grew up in Lafayette Square, an affluent, historic neighborhood near downtown Los Angeles. Within this atmosphere,

---

62 "Taken for Granted: Allyson Felix on Defeating Disappointment and Savoring Success (Transcript)," TED, October 19, 2021, https://www.ted.com/podcasts/worklife/taken-for-granted-allyson-felix-on-defeating-disappointment-and-savoring-success-transcript.

she was exposed to many diverse and successful people. "I always saw people doing amazing things, and that made me feel like things weren't out of reach. It also allowed me to dream,"[63] Allyson said of her childhood. And dream she did. But it may be surprising to know she didn't initially dream of being a world-famous track athlete. Allyson, greatly influenced by her parents and the good they did in the community, wanted to be a teacher.

As a kid, Allyson looked up to her big brother Wes, who was just two years older than she was. They were close companions who enjoyed fun sibling competitions and playing with other neighborhood kids. Some of Allyson's favorite pastimes included basketball, rollerblading, and gymnastics.

She started her high school experience playing basketball at Los Angeles Baptist High. But in the spring of 2000, following in her brother's footsteps as a star track athlete, she decided to try out for the track team to make new friends. At the trials, Allyson stood out from her peers. She clocked the fastest time in the sixty-yard dash and caught the attention of Coach Jonathan Patton. In awe of her time, Patton asked her to run it again. Allyson obliged and delivered the same result. Patton felt there was something special about Allyson and wanted to train her to reach her full potential. From that point on, the direction of Allyson's life changed.

While Patton thought Allyson was special, she wasn't so easily convinced. With her slim physique and long legs, Allyson wasn't muscular or well-defined like the other athletes, which made her self-conscious. She wasn't sure if she fit in with the image she had of what a typical track and field athlete looked like. And it didn't help that her peers teased her with the nickname "chicken legs," only drawing attention to her insecurities.

---

63 Kianoosh Hashemzadeh, "Allyson Felix Is Not Done," USC Rossier, March 29, 2023, https://rossier.usc.edu/news-insights/news/allyson-felix-not-done.

But Allyson soon overcame her doubts. She hit the gym, working to build a strong physique that would carry her through many races. Soon, she could deadlift 270 pounds and much more in her pro career. The extra strength helped improve her speed and power on the track. Allyson left the criticism and doubt behind and concentrated on making the most of her natural abilities.

Within a few months of the tryouts, Allyson participated in her first state track and field meet. She came in seventh place. It was a good beginning, but Allyson could do so much more. She went on to compete in various meets, gaining experience and improving on her results.

In 2001, Allyson won her first state title and came second in the Nike Indoor Nationals. Later that year, she competed in the International Association of Athletics Federation's (IAAF) World Youth Championships in Hungary. It was Allyson's first taste of competition on a global level. She soaked it all in, enjoying the opportunity to make friends and race on an international platform with like-minded young athletes from different countries. In Hungary, she won the 100-meter race. Her Youth Championships experience motivated her to excel and pursue bigger competitions.

As her high school years progressed, Allyson made a name for herself in the track and field world. But it was her run in the Banamex Grand Prix track and field meet in Mexico City on May 3 that catapulted her onto the mainstream. Allyson, now a senior in high school, clocked a time of 22.11 in the 200-meter sprint, setting a new under-twenty world record and breaking Marion Jones's long-standing American junior record. It was a pivotal moment in her career. That year, Allyson was named High School Athlete of the Year by *Track and Field News*. Many had already been paying attention to Allyson, but her record-breaking run put an even greater spotlight on the young athlete.

Allyson was just seventeen, a senior in high school, and the world opened up for her in a new way. She prepared to go to the University of Southern California on a scholarship. But Adidas soon came knocking. In an unprecedented move, Allyson signed a sponsorship contract with the company, making her the first athlete to turn pro out of high school. The deal meant she could not compete on a collegiate level. But she was now a part of Team USA and could compete in professional events.

It was a big decision for Allyson and her family—one they didn't take lightly. Her parents wanted her to continue with her studies and get a degree. Allyson was eager to turn pro, but she also understood the value and importance of education. It was agreed. Allyson would follow through with her plans to attend USC while running track for Team USA. Allyson continued with her studies and went on to obtain a degree in elementary education in 2008.

Allyson's decision to go pro was more than a strategic or financial move. It was a part of a bigger dream. She had her eyes set on the Olympics; the 2004 games were just around the corner. And she knew joining Team USA would give her a head start on her Olympic goals.

PATH TO SUCCESS

In 2004, Allyson made her Olympic debut in Athens, Greece, at age eighteen. She was the youngest member of the US track and field team. But what she lacked in age, she made up for in ability. Lining up with the other racers, Allyson had a look of determination on her face. And when the starting pistol went off, she gave a dynamic push off her block and started taking those long, graceful strides full of pure power she became known for. In the 200-meter race, Allyson won second place. Her time of 22.11 set a new World Junior record. She took home her first Olympic medal, but many more would follow.

Allyson was overwhelmed by her first Olympic experience. There was so much to absorb: events, ceremonies, activities to participate in, and so many people. It was all new to her. And after her race, an inexperienced Allyson missed her victory lap, unaware that all medal winners were expected to walk around the stadium.

Her first experience left an unforgettable mark on Allyson: "I hadn't competed for much internationally at all. I remember just being a teenager and taking it all in. I feel that's what gave me the drive to keep going. It gave me a little taste of it but also showed me that I wasn't there and that there was a lot of work to be done and a lot that goes into this."[64]

Fresh off the heels of her first Olympic games, Allyson participated in another first in 2005, the World Athletics Championships. The games that year were held in Helsinki, Finland. Armed with a new training style and a new coach, Bobby Kersee, husband to the legendary track star Jackie Joyner-Kersee, Allyson felt more prepared than ever. The switch in her routine paid off, and Allyson won the gold in the 200-meter event.

When the World Championships returned in 2007, she dominated the games in Osaka, Japan. She won gold medals in the 200-meter, the 4 x 100, and the 4 x 400 as part of the relay team.

With those wins under her belt, Allyson was confident the 2008 games in Beijing, Japan, would be her year to bring home a gold from the Olympics. But she was edged out in mere milliseconds in the 200-meter run by Veronica Campbell-Brown, one of her

---

64 Stuart Weir, "28 Questions to Allyson Felix, from the *RunBlogRun* Archives," *RunBlogRun*, October 21, 2022, https://www.runblogrun.com/2022/10/28 -questions-to-allyson-felix-december-2018-from-the-runblogrun-archives.html.

greatest rivals. So, while Allyson won the silver medal, it wasn't what she had hoped or trained so hard for. The second-place win fell flat, and she was visibly disappointed. She would, however, go on to earn gold with the relay team, who won the 4 x 400.

Her near results in the 2008 games showed Allyson that she still had more work to do to win a gold medal at the Olympics. Together with her coach, she reevaluated her tactics and changed everything from how she exercised to how she launched out of the starting block. But would it pay off?

In between her Olympic appearances, Allyson upheld her World Championship title, winning the gold medal in the 200 meters in both 2007 and 2009 events.

When the Olympic Games returned in 2012 in London, England, Allyson proved that giving up on her dream was not an option. She reigned supreme in the games as both an individual sprinter and a team player. With the help of her new training, Allyson finally won the elusive gold medal in the 200-meter sprint. With her time of 21.88 seconds, she beat out stiff competition in Shelly-Ann Fraser-Pryce, who was only .21 seconds slower, and Carmelita Jeter, who came in third. Allyson was elated. "It's been a long time coming. I am so overjoyed. I thought back to the disappointment in Beijing, it's been a long road, I never wanted to give up. I've wanted it for so long. This moment is really priceless,"[65] she said of her win. The relay team went on to win gold in the 4 x 100 and 4 x 400 events.

Allyson and the US relay team were back in the 2016 Olympics in Rio de Janeiro, Brazil. By then, Allyson had also started running the 400 meters. The team took home the gold again in the 4 x 100

---

65 Mark Trevelyan and Mike Collett-White, "U.S. Reigns on Track and Beach," *Reuters*, August 8, 2012, https://www.reuters.com/article/us-oly-wrap-day12 -idUSBRE87702H20120808.

and the 4 x 400 events, making Allyson the first female athlete to earn six Olympic gold medals. Allyson also won silver in the 400 meters that year.

In 2017, Allyson became the most decorated athlete in the World Championships, with a career total of sixteen medals. The games were held in London, England. Allyson received the bronze for her performance in the 400-meter event.

At the 2020 games in Tokyo, Japan, Allyson's final Olympics, she ran the fastest 400 meter in her career with a time of 49.46 seconds. She took home the bronze medal in the 400 meter, and the relay team won gold in the 4 x 400 relay. For Allyson, her final bronze Olympic medal was the most meaningful. She had come a long way from the shy, insecure girl who had started running in ninth grade.

When it was all said and done, Allyson had eleven Olympic and twenty World Championship medals to her name. She broke Carl Lewis's record of ten Olympic medals and surpassed Usain Bolt's fourteen World Championship medals. She was now the most decorated athlete in track and field history, male or female.

TRIALS AND TRIBULATIONS

Among her incredible highs, Allyson has experienced many lows as well. Injuries have set her back on a few occasions, most notably in the 2013 World Championships in Moscow, where a hamstring injury caused her to collapse in the middle of the race. Her brother and agent, Wes, always her biggest supporter, carried her off the track. It was a humbling moment for her—one she counts as the low point of her career. It was her first major injury, and it made her question everything. But her brother helped her put it into perspective, telling her, "How long have you been running?

How many injuries have you had and come back from? This is just something that is going to be a part of your journey."[66] Allyson listened to her brother, took time to heal, and returned to seize the World Championships in 2014.

Another significant injury in April 2016 almost stopped Allyson from taking part in the 2016 Olympics, which were taking place in July. While performing an exercise in the gym, Allyson tore the ligaments in her right ankle. It would be a long road to recovery from there. And Allyson felt she had jeopardized her chances at the Olympics, which were just around the corner. She had hoped to qualify for both the 200- and 400-meter sprints. In true Allyson style, though, she battled back, opting to choose therapy over surgery. And while she made the 400-meter team, her injury affected her performance in the 200-meter tryouts. The hope of running both events was over. Nevertheless, at the games, she went on to win silver in the 400 meter and gold with the relay team.

Allyson was always her own biggest critic, always looking to do better than she'd done before. And sometimes, that clouded her ability to see how much she achieved. In the 2008 Olympic games, though she won silver, she felt defeated. She thought she was poised to take home the gold, but she felt she underperformed. It was a crushing blow, but one that would teach her a valuable lesson about losing. "I learned much more than if I had won that race, you know, it's, it's so much more valuable. I had to kind of look at everything I was doing, reevaluate everything, figure out like, can I, is there any way that I can get better at my craft? And I looked at nutrition, weightlifting, coaching, you know, all those

66 Allyson Felix, "Always There by Allyson Felix | The Players' Tribune," The Players' Tribune, August 6, 2021, https://www.theplayerstribune.com/articles/allyson-felix-olympics-brother.

things, but it was that moment that brought me to it. And I think it's that, that moment that allowed me to get better from it."[67]

Two of Allyson's biggest challenges came off the field and would shape how she moved forward with her career. Back in 2010, Allyson signed a sponsorship deal with Nike, ending her time with Adidas. Allyson became one of Nike's most marketable representatives. But things changed when she wanted to start a family. With her contract up for renewal in 2017, she found the company would not extend maternal protection to her nor provide compensation if she got pregnant. Allyson spoke out about the mistreatment, leading to a public outcry. Personally, Allyson was incredibly hurt by Nike's stance on the issue. She had been with Nike for a long time, and their unwillingness to change felt like a betrayal of their relationship and an insult to all female athletes. Allyson parted ways with the brand. Her advocacy led to the shoe company adopting a new maternal policy for sponsored athletes in 2019. And Allyson created her own athletic shoe line specifically catered to women.

In 2018, Allyson gave birth to her daughter, Camryn. But toward the end of her pregnancy, she found out she had severe preeclampsia, a serious condition that put her life and the life of her baby at risk. She had to have an emergency C-section, and her baby had to spend a month in the intensive care unit of the hospital. It was a scary and stressful time for Allyson, made worse by Nike's refusal to grant her maternity rights. The experience led Allyson to become an advocate and speaker on maternal health issues, especially those facing Black women.

Ten months after Allyson recuperated from the birth of her child, she was back on the racing track. She trained hard during her

---

67 "Taken for Granted," TED.

absence and came back ready to show everyone she was not yet done with track and field. Allyson and the relay team won gold in the 4 x 400 at the 2019 World Championships in Doha, Qatar. She took home the bronze medal in the 400 meter, as well. It was a triumphant, full-circle moment for Allyson, who did it all wearing the shoes she had created.

ACHIEVEMENTS

Allyson has had a monumental career in track and field, spanning almost two decades, and she only recently called it quits. Starting with her early wins in high school, Allyson burst onto the scene, leaving no doubt she was headed for bigger things. From the age of seventeen to the age of thirty-six, she has amassed a collection of awards and achievements that are unparalleled.

She has participated in five Olympic games and has come home as a medal winner in each one. Whether running in an individual event or on the Team USA relay, Allyson put in the work and was rewarded for it. As an individual sprinter, she won the gold medal in the 2012 games in London, three silver medals in the 2004, 2008, and 2016 games, and the bronze medal in the 2020 games.

With Allyson on board, Team USA has won numerous relay events, including gold in the 4 x 400 in the 2008, 2012, 2016, and 2020 games. Additionally, they won gold in the 4 x 100 category in 2012 and 2016.

Allyson has dominated the World Championship games since participating in them in 2005. She has won nineteen World Championship medals, including fourteen gold, three silver, and two bronze.

Allyson's last competition, a mixed 4 x 400 relay, was at the World Championships in Eugene, Oregon, on July 15, 2022. When she took the baton from her teammate, the crowd roared with excitement, showing their appreciation for the beloved sprinter. She felt the outpouring from the crowd, and it warmed her heart and spurred her on to hear the cheers. Allyson and her teammates managed to secure a third-place finish, ensuring she left the sport on a high with a bronze medal.

But of all the races and medals she's achieved, Allyson says her last Olympics holds a special place for her. "Winning that bronze medal, it was so special. I was so happy to be able to do so with my daughter in mind, but with so many women and moms in mind as well, and just overcoming so much. So that was incredible. And then to get to run on the relay and get the gold medal, and that was so special. . . . I couldn't have dreamt it any better."[68]

LIFE LESSONS

When she started out, Allyson didn't fit the mold of your typical track star. And while that could have held her back or made her change sports altogether, she stuck with it, using her uniqueness to her advantage. Those "chicken legs" made her the most powerful sprinter in the world. She showed that it's often our differences that make us special.

Allyson has handled every situation with grace. Through the ups and downs, whether winning or losing, she proves that character is built in the toughest of times. How we persevere, problem solve, and get back up after being knocked down can teach us so much about ourselves and our capabilities.

Allyson has had to fight back many times, and each time she did, she showed that past mistakes or disappointments do not define you. We can reinvent ourselves and keep moving toward

---

68 "Taken for Granted," TED.

our goals, even if they look different from when we started. When people counted her out after the birth of her daughter, she went on to compete in more races and ended her career when she was ready. When her training wasn't working, she changed it up and reaped the benefits.

Allyson was always bold in pushing herself to the next level. Her resilience, discipline, and work ethic made her a household name in America and worldwide. She wasn't afraid to use her voice and platform to advocate for and bring attention to important issues facing female athletes and Black mothers. Though she recently left the sport, she left behind an enduring legacy that will inspire many generations to come.

ALICE COACHMAN

"To be a champion, you got to have determination, you've got to have guts; you have to train and let nothing come between you and what you want, that goal you want to reach."[69]

EARLY YEARS

Would you believe the first African American woman to win a gold medal in track and field at the Olympics started out jumping over sticks and running barefoot along the roadside? Alice Coachman didn't have access to facilities, equipment, or even running shoes, but she made do with what she had and high jumped her way into history.

Alice grew up in Albany, Georgia, where she was born on November 9, 1923. She was the fifth in a big family of five girls and five boys. Her father, a plasterer, and her mother, a maid, worked hard to support their large family. But times were tough, and the family was poor. All the children, including Alice, had to help their parents make ends meet. To earn extra money, the family worked at a nearby plantation, picking cotton, peaches, peanuts, and whatever was in harvest.

Family life in the Coachman home centered around the church and adhering to a rigid moral code. Alice's parents were strict,

---

69 Miles Educational Film Productions, "Interview with Alice Coachman," Washington University in St. Louis, last accessed June 18, 2024, http://repository .wustl.edu/concern/videos/b27740880.

deeply religious, and had strong beliefs about the way young girls should conduct themselves. As a fun-loving girl who liked music, sports, and playing with boys, Alice challenged all of her parents' beliefs, and she would often get in trouble for disobeying their rules.

From early on, Alice was defiant and strong-willed—characteristics that would be useful later in her life. Growing up, Alice loved to dance and dreamed of being a saxophone player or tap dancer like her favorite entertainers. But she was punished anytime her parents caught her dancing. Likewise, she loved playing games outside with her friends. She liked to run, skip, and jump like most kids do and play softball and baseball with the boys. But playing sports and spending time with boys only resulted in more punishment for Alice. But no matter how much trouble she got into, she'd go back out and do it again.

Alice especially liked hanging with boys. They treated her like one of them. In a time when girls were expected to be dainty and quiet, Alice was far from conventional. She could be competitive and strong with the boys, who accepted her as she was.

Alice went to school at Monroe Street Elementary School. During breaks, the kids at the school would have competitions on the playground to see who could run the fastest or the farthest, or jump highest. And the boys especially liked to tease Alice that she couldn't beat them. She always took them up on the challenge. And she always bested them.

Because of segregation, the law that separated whites from Blacks and denied African Americans equal treatment, the children didn't have access to training facilities or sports equipment. But Alice and her friends were smart. They learned to make what they needed from what they had. They used sticks, ropes, or materials to make crossbars they could jump over. And with no one to train her, Alice learned to coach herself. To improve her running, she often ran along the roadside barefoot.

While Alice happily ran and jumped with her friends, she caught the attention of Cora Bailey, her fifth-grade teacher. Bailey strongly supported Alice and encouraged her to keep running and join a team when the opportunity arose. The thoughtful encouragement gave Alice confidence and helped her continue along this unconventional path.

Alice took her teacher's advice to heart and immediately joined the track team when she started seventh grade at Madison High School. Along with running, she took a serious interest in the high jump. But with no training facilities and limited resources available to Black youth, she continued to practice on her own using makeshift crossbars and jumping over fences.

Harry Lash, the football coach at Madison High School, saw her potential and helped train her. In May, an opportunity arose for Alice to compete at Tuskegee Institute, and Lash arranged for her to participate. The Tuskegee Institute was a prominent higher education school for Black children in Alabama. It was a big step to take Alice there. Lash was hesitant because Alice was still a little young for the competitions, which were typically held for participants in grades eight to twelve. But Lash knew she was better than many and couldn't let the opportunity pass. At the Tuskegee meet, Alice broke the high school and college records. The Tuskegee coaches were so impressed they asked her to come and join the track team and travel with them in the summer to the Amateur Athletic Union (AAU) National Championships in Waterbury, Connecticut.

The AAU meet was her first trip so far away from home and out of the South. At the competition, Alice set a new American record. Tuskegee offered Alice a working scholarship and asked her to join the school and continue her education there. But Alice's parents weren't happy. They didn't want her to go away to Tuskegee, and they had never approved of her running and jumping. They thought sports were dangerous and unladylike. They said no. But Alice was adamant. She wanted to go and said, "Well, I'm going anyway."[70]

And with that defiant stance, her parents gave in. She didn't know what was ahead of her, but she knew there were so many possibilities.

Alice attended the AAU championships in the summer of 1939, just before she started at Tuskegee. And she did better than good at the events. At just sixteen years old, she set a new American high school and college record in the high jump, all while competing in bare feet. Alice was the National Championship winner. She was excited. It was a great start to a new chapter of her life.

The head coach at Tuskegee, Cleveland "Cleve" Abbott, was very strict. But Alice was used to a strict household, so Abbott's rules didn't faze her. Training and beating her competition, she stayed focused on her studies at Tuskegee.

PATH TO SUCCESS

Alice settled into life at Tuskegee. It became her home away from home, and during her time at the school, she would take her love of running and jumping to a whole new level.

---

70 "Interview with Alice Coachman," Washington University in St. Louis.

She had to work her way through Tuskegee, as her parents didn't have the money to help her pay for her room and board. So, she took jobs around campus wherever they were available to support her stay. Alice was incredibly busy; besides working, she was on the women's track and field team and the basketball team, where she played guard. Alice and her teammates won three basketball conference titles during her time at Tuskegee. She also joined the school choir, which became a great escape from the pressures of her routine.

Tuskegee's reputation as a leading school for Black people exposed Alice to many accomplished Black artists, musicians, activists, and elites of the time who came through the school. That exposure gave Alice a taste of what was possible and helped her dream bigger dreams than she would've ever had back home. She decided she wanted to be famous and would work hard to get there.

As it turns out, Alice's first AAU high jump championship in 1939 was just the beginning of a remarkable decade for her in track and field. For the next ten years, she outjumped all her competitors and reigned supreme as the national AAU champion. But her command of the sport wasn't limited to the high jump. Alice was just as powerful a runner as she was a jumper. She participated in the 50-meter dash, the 100-meter dash, and the 400-meter relay with her team. And she won titles in all three events.

Alice had a unique approach to the sport of high jumping. Because she was initially self-taught, she developed her own way of jumping, a cross between the western roll and the scissors techniques, two traditional styles of the high jump. But the unusual combination served her well and helped her win many events. Alice also developed a quirky habit of bringing lemons to the track meets. She would suck on them when she needed something to energize her. "And when my mouth got tired and dry on the inside, I would squeeze a little of that lemon, and it kept me light."[71] The practice became a superstition or good luck charm for her. At every event, she always had a lucky lemon with her.

Alice enjoyed her time at Tuskegee, and despite her busy athletic schedule, she made time for her studies, graduating with a degree in dressmaking. In 1947, Alice decided to further her studies at Albany State College, majoring in economics and minoring in science. While at Albany, Alice continued her run as a track and field champion, earning additional titles for her performance in her areas of expertise: the high jump and the 50- and 100-meter dashes.

With the 1948 Olympics approaching, many people urged Alice to compete in the tryouts. As the national track and field champion, she would surely be able to secure a spot on the Olympic team.

Alice took their advice and decided to try out. On July 12, 1948, Alice surpassed everyone's expectations at the tryouts. With her jump of 5 feet, 4 3/4 inches, she not only came in first in the long jump but also broke a long-standing record. Known for keeping her cool, Alice was unfazed by her placement in the tryouts. She said, "I was never nervous because I didn't talk. I just had a lemon and stretched out."[72] With her spot on the Olympic team secured, all Alice had left to do was prepare. The Summer Olympics were less than a month away.

She returned to Albany hoping to prepare for the games there but was disappointed to find out she wasn't allowed to train at the whites-only facilities. Thankfully, she could return to Tuskegee, which was well-equipped, to complete her training.

---

71 "Interview with Alice Coachman," Washington University in St. Louis.
72 "Interview with Alice Coachman," Washington University in St. Louis.

In the summer of 1948, Alice was on her way to the Olympic games in London, England. The team traveled by boat to England, an awe-inspiring experience for Alice. It was also Alice's first time traveling to Europe. She liked the thrill and beauty of the open water and the opportunity to meet new people. And she was happy she didn't get seasick like some of her teammates, so she got to fully enjoy the adventure. When they got to London, Alice was surprised to see she was a bit of a celebrity there. As it turned out, the British were more interested in track and field than Americans, and Alice's reputation as an outstanding athlete was well known. Many people were eager to see her compete.

On August 7, 1948, on a cloudy day in London, Alice Coachman followed her dreams all the way to Olympic gold. In her classic style, she wasn't worried about the event. "I've always believed that I could do whatever I set my mind to do; I've had that strong will, that oneness of purpose, all my life. That morning, I knew I had the ability."[73] All Alice needed was her trusty lemon, which she used to refresh herself between jumps and her belief in her higher purpose.

In the high jump finals competition, she cleared 5 feet, 6 1/8 inches on her first try, outjumping her closest competition, Dorothy Tyler. With that jump, she set a new world record, becoming the first African American woman from any country to win a gold medal in the Olympics and the only American woman to bring home a gold medal for those games.

But Alice didn't even know she had won until she looked up on the leaderboard. And when she did, she found her name at the very top. It was a surreal moment. Everything moved so quickly. She still hadn't processed her win by the time she was led to

---

73 Shirelle Phelps and Gale Research Inc., *Contemporary Black Biography Vol. 18: Profiles from the International Black Community* (Detroit, MI: Gale, 1998).

the podium. But when they played the American anthem in the packed stadium, Alice felt nothing but pride.

The King of England, King George VI, awarded Alice her medal, and she was treated to a special tour of England. She was in awe of meeting King George and enjoyed touring a city unlike those she knew. But what she noticed most was how socially different the town was. There was no segregation there, and Black and white people lived side by side.

Back home, Alice got to bask in her celebrity for a time. She was invited to the White House, where she met President Harry Truman and was thrown a party by the great jazz artist Count Basie. It was a lot of fun for Alice.

TRIALS AND TRIBULATIONS

Though Alice was at the top of her game during her college years, she couldn't go further than the national level because of circumstances outside her control. World War II broke out in 1939 and lasted six long years, wreaking havoc on countries all over the world. Many lives were lost, and all non-wartime activities ceased. As a result, the Olympics were canceled in 1940 and again in 1944.

Despite her outstanding performance stateside and the encouragement of her supporters, competing in the games wasn't possible in those years. It was disappointing for her, but she could do nothing about it. She would surely have brought home multiple medals if the Olympics had occurred. "Had she competed in those canceled Olympics, we would probably be talking about her as the No. 1 female athlete of all time,"[74] Eric Williams of the Black Athlete Sports Network wrote.

As a Black woman, Alice witnessed discrimination and racism up close, especially growing up in the segregated South. Even after she won gold at the Olympics, her accomplishments were downplayed by some American press outlets. The news that she was the first Black woman to win an Olympic gold didn't get the recognition it should have.

And when she returned to Albany, segregation tainted her reception. While the town celebrated her win with a city-wide parade, she still had to suffer through the indignities of discrimination. At the ceremony to honor her achievement, Alice, along with the other Black people in attendance, were treated like second-class citizens, as was customary of the time. The mayor, while congratulatory, would not shake her hand, a slight Alice would never forget. In the auditorium, Blacks were separated from whites and had to sit in a designated area. And Alice wasn't even allowed to use the front entrance of the building where they were celebrating her. Instead, she had to use the back door.

ACCOMPLISHMENTS

After her win at the Olympics, Alice retired from track and field. She was only twenty-five years old. Though she may have been able to compete for a few more years, Alice felt it was time to call it quits. "I had accomplished what I wanted to do. . . . That was the climax. I won the gold medal. I proved to my mother, my father,

---

[74] Alan Greenblatt, "Why an African-American Sports Pioneer Remains Obscure," NPR, July 19, 2014, https://www.npr.org/sections/codeswitch/2014/07/19/332665921/why-an-african-american-sports-pioneer-remains-obscure.

my coach and everybody else that I had gone to the end of my rope,"[75] she said.

Though her flame burned only for a short time, it burned bright. Alice is still considered one of the greatest track and field athletes. In total, she collected twenty-five national titles between 1939 and 1948, most famously winning the National AAU high jump championship every year for ten years straight.

Additionally, during that decade, Alice also won the 50-meter outdoor championships for five straight years from 1943 to 1947 and the indoor 50-meter dash in 1945 and 1946. She also won the title for the 100-meter dash in 1942, 1945, and 1946.

She was the only African American to be named to five All-American teams for the 50-meter, 100-meter, 400-meter, and 50-yard dashes and national relay teams.

Her biggest achievement, of course, was the Olympic games on August 7, 1948, when she won gold for her jump and set a new Olympic and American record on that day. She was also the only woman to bring home a gold medal and the first Black woman to win gold at the Olympics.

As a testament to Alice's legacy, she has been inducted into many Halls of Fame, including the National Track and Field Hall of Fame in 1975. In 2004, she was inducted into the US Olympic and Paralympic Hall of Fame. Other inductions include the Black Athletes Hall of Fame, the Georgia State Hall of Fame, and the Tuskegee Hall of Fame. She was also honored at the 1996 Summer Olympic Games as one of the 100 greatest Olympians in history.

75 "Alice Coachman, Who Won a Gold Medal but Came Home to Segregation," *The New York Times*, August 19, 2016, https://www.nytimes.com/interactive /projects/cp/obituaries/archives/alice-coachman.

At a time when there were only a few Black athletes in sports, Alice helped further the cause for equality with her triumphant performances. Because of the doors she opened, Alice showed Americans that Black people could compete on the national and world stage and win.

Alice was proud of her achievements and what it would mean for those who would come after her. "I made a difference among the blacks, being one of the leaders. If I had gone to the Games and failed, there wouldn't be anyone to follow in my footsteps. It encouraged the rest of the women to work harder and fight harder."[76]

Even after her retirement, Alice continued to make significant strides for female athletes. In 1952, she became the first female athlete to earn an endorsement deal, becoming a spokesperson for Coca-Cola.

LIFE LESSONS

Alice died July 14, 2014, in her hometown of Albany, where she had taught as a teacher for many years. The track and field community lost a pioneer and legend that day. And her inspirational story shows us how to become the best at anything we dream of doing.

Alice was self-determined and knew what she wanted at an early age. Once she set her sights on a goal, she achieved it and wasn't deterred by any obstacles. Even though segregation denied her access to resources and facilities, she persevered. And though the war postponed her rise to stardom, she still reached the top of

76 "Alice Coachman, 90, Dies; First Black Woman to Win Olympic Gold," *The New York Times*, July 15, 2014, https://www.nytimes.com/2014/07/15/sports/alice-coachman-90-dies-groundbreaking-medalist.html.

the podium. From Alice, we can learn it's not what you have; it's what you do with what you have that matters.

Alice could have given up her dream at any time, but she didn't. When her parents said no, when resources were unavailable or circumstances were stacked against her, she believed she could. So she did. A love for the sport and a need to prove herself kept Alice committed to what she started.

With a winning state of mind and a can-do attitude, Alice reached as far as she dared to dream and beyond. Alice said it best in her own words: "I've always believed that I could do whatever I set my mind to do. I've always had that strong will, that oneness of purpose, all my life."[77]

Do you have what it takes to follow your dreams?

---

[77] Shirelle Phelps and Gale Research Inc., *Contemporary Black Biography Vol. 18.*

THE FINAL TAKEAWAY

What can these inspiring stories about Black athletes tell you about following your dreams? Everyone reading this may take away something different. But at the heart of each story is an underlying theme: success is a journey, but it's a journey worth taking.

Along the path you will encounter obstacles, disappointments, and challenges. But, as we learned from each of these sports legends, success is determined by how you navigate those difficulties. Your circumstances do not define you, whatever they may be. If you stay determined, you can push through and overcome anything.

Trailblazing African American athletes from the past shattered color barriers when times were toughest. They were the first to make a stand, cross into unknown territories, and endure some of the worst treatment. They had no one who looked like them to admire or emulate. And despite the obstacles that were stacked against them, they found the courage to follow their dreams wherever they took them. They achieved greatness in a time when African Americans were not even considered equals.

Many have followed in the footsteps of these athletic pioneers and have kept up their legacy of greatness. Today, Black athletes continue to make inroads in sports, break records, and establish long-lasting legacies. They come from all backgrounds and situations and have shown that commitment, determination, and a positive mindset are the greatest assets any athlete and young achiever can possess.

These motivational success stories have also shown us there will be times when you question yourself, your abilities, and whether you belong. Being afraid is okay; being unsure is okay. If you put in the work, stick to your plan, and seize opportunities, confidence will follow. And when you believe in yourself, anything is possible.

You may wonder why you should follow your dreams. What's on the other side of all the hard work, anyway? The answer is a life full of meaning, happiness, fulfillment, and an indescribable feeling of accomplishment. Remember to follow your heart, do your best, and stay true to yourself.

Your dreams are worth following!

REFERENCES

CHAPTER 1: TENNIS

SERENA WILLIAMS

Britannica, s.v. "Serena Williams." Accessed September 27, 2023. https://www.britannica.com/biography/Serena-Williams.

Hess, Liam. "The 9 Greatest Moments of Serena Williams's Tennis Career." *Vogue*. August 9, 2022. https://www.vogue.com/article/9-greatest-moments-serena-williams-tennis-career.

Jiwani, Rory. "Serena Williams—Tennis Career Statistics and Facts." *Olympics*. May 2, 2023. https://olympics.com/en/news/tennis-serena-williams-career-statistics-facts.

Murali, Mahalakshmi. "You Have to Believe in Yourself When No One Else Does—Serena Williams Addresses Class of 2020 at Mouratoglou's Academy." EssentiallySports. July 7, 2020. https://www.essentiallysports.com/tennis-news-wta-you-have-to-believe-in-yourself-when-no-one-else-does-serena-williams-addresses-class-of-2020-at-mouratoglous-academy.

US Open Tennis Championships. "Serena Williams Press Conference | 2022 US Open Round 3." YouTube. September 3, 2022. https://www.youtube.com/watch?v=abJFrMOyqPM.

Williams, Richard. *Black and White: The Way I See It*. New York: Atria Books, 2014.

Williams, Serena. "How Serena Williams Saved Her Own Life." *ELLE*. April 5, 2022. https://www.elle.com/life-love/a39586444/how-serena-williams-saved-her-own-life.

Williams, Serena, and Daniel Paisner. *Queen of the Court*. New York: Simon & Schuster, 2009.

ALTHEA GIBSON

Britannica, s.v. "Althea Gibson." Accessed October 19, 2023. https://www.britannica.com/biography/Althea-Gibson.

Donnelly, Marea. "Colour No Barrier for Self-Centred Champion." *The Daily Telegraph*. July 5, 2017. https://www.dailytelegraph.com.au/news /althea-gibson-broke-wimbledon-colour-barrier-with-first-singles-win /news-story/cc7f8c70848e2fa2bbe7fe7587cedb37.

Gibson, Althea, Edward E. Fitzgerald, and Stephen M. Joseph. *I Always Wanted to Be Somebody*. New York: Noble and Noble, 1970.

Knight, Christina. "Althea Gibson Biographical Timeline." PBS. April 25, 2022. https://www.pbs.org/wnet/americanmasters/althea-althea -gibson-timeline/5393.

"The ATA Has a Rich History." American Tennis Association. Accessed March 18, 2024. https://www.yourata.org/history.

"'The Most Important Pioneer for Tennis'—Althea Gibson's Great Legacy." Women's Tennis Association. August 25, 2020. https://www.wtatennis .com/news/1739180/the-most-important-pioneer-for-tennis-althea -gibson-s-great-legacy.

CHAPTER 2: BASEBALL

AARON JUDGE

"Aaron Judge of New York Yankees Ties Mark McGwire for Home Runs by Rookie." ESPN. September 25, 2017. https://www.espn.com/mlb/story /_/id/20816622/aaron-judge-new-york-yankees-ties-mark-mcgwire -home-runs-rookie.

Casaletto, Lucas. "Aaron Judge: 'I Wouldn't Be a New York Yankee If It Wasn't for My Mom.'" The Score. December 8, 2023. https://www .thescore.com/mlb/news/1300236.

FOX Sports. "J. P. Morosi Sits Down with Yankees Star, Aaron Judge | FOX MLB." YouTube. August 3, 2019. https://www.youtube.com /watch?v=sSOb2uq5IqA.

Grant, Tracy. "Aaron Judge." *Britannica*. Accessed December 7, 2023. https://www.britannica.com/biography/Aaron-Judge.

Hoch, Bryan. *62: Aaron Judge, the New York Yankees, and the Pursuit of Greatness*. New York: Atria Books, 2024.

"Judge on Breaking AL Home Run Record." MLB. October 5, 2022. https://www.mlb.com/video/judge-on-breaking-al-home-run-record.

Kernan, Kevin. "Aaron Judge's Star Power Is Slump-Proof for Now." *New York Post*. August 14, 2017. https://nypost.com/2017/08/14/aaron-judge-takes-another-giant-leap-toward-superstardom.

Matz, Eddie. "Hop in the Back, Mom and Dad Are Driving! What It's Really Like Getting Called up to the Majors." ESPN. August 30, 2019. https://www.espn.com/mlb/story/_/id/27468317/hop-back-mom-dad-driving-really-getting-called-majors.

Rosa, Francisco. "Yankees' Aaron Judge Wins 2023 Roberto Clemente Award Honoring Community Involvement." *Bleacher Report*. October 30, 2023. https://bleacherreport.com/articles/10095442-yankees-aaron-Aaron-wins-2023-roberto-clemente-award-honoring-community-involvement.

Simon, Andrew. "Explaining the MLB Farm System." MLB. February 16, 2023. https://www.mlb.com/news/the-mlb-farm-system-explained.

Verducci, Tom. "Aaron Judge: The Authentic Home Run King." *Sports Illustrated*. October 5, 2022. https://www.si.com/mlb/2022/10/05/aaron-judge-authentic-home-run-king.

JACKIE ROBINSON

"9 Quotes about Jackie Robinson." JackieRobinson.org. January 19, 2018. https://jackierobinson.org/news/9-quotes-about-jackie-robinson.

Britannica, s.v. "Jackie Robinson." Accessed December 20, 2023. https://www.britannica.com/biography/Jackie-Robinson.

"Robinson, Jackie | Baseball Hall of Fame." Baseball Hall of Fame. Accessed March 18, 2024. https://baseballhall.org/hall-of-famers/robinson-jackie.

Robinson, Jackie. *I Never Had It Made: An Autobiography of Jackie Robinson*. New York: Harper Collins, 1995.

CHAPTER 3: BASKETBALL

LEBRON JAMES

Aim Arena. "Lebron James Reveals His Top 5 Tips for Conquering Hard Work." YouTube. November 11, 2023. https://www.youtube.com /watch?v=f2xrJsEP82U.

Augustyn, Adam. "LeBron James." *Britannica*. Accessed February 15, 2024. https://www.britannica.com/biography/LeBron-James.

EntreXpreneur. "This Is Lebron James | Motivation from LeBron James." YouTube. December 27, 2021. https://www.youtube.com /watch?v=4DfVOHaD67A.

Hughes, Grant. "How LeBron James Can Fulfill His Dream of Being NBA's Greatest Ever." *Bleacher Report*. August 21, 2013. https://bleacherreport. com/articles/1745816-how-lebron-james-can-fulfill-his-dream-of-being -nbas-greatest-ever.

James, Steve. *LeBron James: The Inside Story of How LeBron James Became King James of The Court*. Scotts Valley, CA: CreateSpace Independent Publishing Platform, 2017.

"LeBron James Points Tracker: NBA's All-time Top Scorer Nears 48,000 Career Points." *Olympics*. Last updated February 14, 2024. https://olympics.com/en/news/lebron-james-points-tracker-nba-all -time-top-scorer.

"LeBron James Staying with the Cavaliers: 'I Love It Here in Cleveland.'" *The Guardian*. June 22, 2016. https://www.theguardian.com/sport/2016 /jun/22/lebron-james-staying-cleveland-cavaliers-nba.

Murphy, David. "21 People Who Made LeBron James the Man He Is Today." *Bleacher Report*. October 3, 2017. https://bleacherreport.com /articles/1876553-21-people-who-made-lebron-james-the-man-he-is -today.

Windhorst, Brian. "In Their Own Words: How the Legendary 2003 NBA Draft Shaped Basketball's Future." ESPN. May 22, 2023. https://www .espn.com/nba/story/_/id/35799683/oral-history-2023-nba-draft -lottery-lebron-james-carmelo-anthony-chris-bosh-dwyane-wade.

Wahl, Grant. "Ahead of His Class." *Sports Illustrated*. August 16, 2022. https://vault.si.com/vault/2002/02/18/ahead-of-his-class-ohio-high

-school-junior-lebron-james-is-so-good-that-hes-already-being
-mentioned-as-the-heir-to-air-jordan.

EARL FRANCIS LLOYD

"1954–55 Syracuse Nationals Roster and Stats." Accessed March 18, 2024. https://www.basketball-reference.com/teams/SYR/1955.html#all_per _game-playoffs_per_game.

Britannica, s.v. "Earl Lloyd." Accessed December 3, 2004. https://www.britannica.com/biography/Earl-Lloyd.

Dow, Bill. "Former Piston Earl Lloyd Recalls Breaking the NBA Color Barrier." Vintage Detroit Collection. February 28, 2015. https://www .vintagedetroit.com/former-piston-earl-lloyd-recalls-breaking-the-nba -color-barrier.

"Earl Lloyd | Syracuse Nationals." NBA. Accessed March 18, 2024. https://www.nba.com/stats/player/77394/career.

"Earl Francis Lloyd." TheHistoryMakers.com. Accessed March 18, 2024. https://www.thehistorymakers.org/biography/earl-francis-lloyd-41.

Lloyd, Earl, and Sean Peter Kirst. *Moonfixer: The Basketball Journey of Earl Lloyd*. Syracuse, NY: Syracuse University Press, 2011.

CHAPTER 4: FOOTBALL

RUSSELL WILSON

Boyle, John. "Bobby Wagner Named 2023 Steve Largent Award Winner." Seahawks. January 1, 2024. https://www.seahawks.com/news/bobby -wagner-named-2023-steve-largent-award-winner.

Brown, James, and Alvin Patrick. "Russell Wilson: The Seattle Seahawks Quarterback Wants to Have an Impact on Youth Far Beyond the Gridiron." *CBS News*. September 8, 2019. https://www.cbsnews.com /news/seattle-seahawks-qb-russell-wilson-why-not-you.

Cash, Meredith. "Photos From Every Year of Russell Wilson's Outstanding NFL Career—From His Seattle Success to Struggles in Denver." *Business Insider*. November 19, 2023. https://www.businessinsider.com/russell -wilson-nfl-career-by-year-2023-11.

Henderson, Brady. "'Why Not You?' Late Father Still Inspires Seattle Seahawks' Russell Wilson—ESPN." ESPN. August 4, 2020. https://www

.espn.com/nfl/story/_/id/29573631/why-not-late-father-inspires
-seahawks-russell-wilson.

Heyen, Billy. "Did Russell Wilson Play Baseball? Yes, and the Yankees Still
Own His MLB Draft Rights." *Sporting News*. September 18, 2021.
https://www.sportingnews.com/us/nfl/news/russell-wilson-baseball-yan
kees/1hikem8pq2901szk59gy9xmnb.

Parrilla, Uriel. "Which Quarterbacks Have More Than 100 Wins?" *Diario
AS*. September 17, 2022. https://en.as.com/nfl/which-quarterbacks-have
-more-than-100-wins-n.

"Parting Words from Russell Wilson." Collegiate School. July 13, 2007.
https://www.collegiate-va.org/news-detail?pk=399055.

Rastogi, Rishi. "Analysis: 4 Moments Where Russell Wilson Showed Early
Signs of Greatness with Seahawks," *Sports Illustrated Seattle Seahawks
News, Analysis and More*. March 30, 2022. https://www.si.com/nfl
/seahawks/gm-report/analysis-4-moments-where-russell-wilson
-showed-early-signs-of-greatness-with-seahawks#gid=ci029d73979000
2731&pid=2-wilson-mounts-an-improbable-comeback-in-his-second
-career-playoff-game.

Rudman, Steve. "Super Bowl Interception Still Haunts Wilson."
Sportspress Northwest. February 20, 2015. https://www.sportspressnw
.com/2198735/2015/wilson-steps-up-takes-blame-for-super-bowl-loss.

"Russell Wilson." Denver Broncos. Accessed March 18, 2024. https://www
.denverbroncos.com/team/players-roster/russell-wilson/career.

"The Childhood, Family, and Faith Behind Seahawk Russell Wilson."
MyNorthwest. January 10, 2013. https://mynorthwest.com/5569/the
-childhood-family-and-faith-behind-seahawk-russell-wilson.

The Richmond Forum. "Russell Wilson With Dr. Henry Louis Gates, Jr. at
the Richmond Forum." YouTube. April 18, 2016. https://www.youtube
.com/watch?v=4aZCBlL8P6U.

Waleik, Gary. "Fritz Pollard: The Small Running Back Who Broke Big
Barriers | Only a Game." WBUR. January 12, 2018. https://www.wbur.org
/onlyagame/2018/01/12/fritz-pollard-football.

FRITZ POLLARD

Carroll, John M. "Fritz Pollard | NFL Pioneer, African American Trailblazer." *Britannica*. Accessed January 23, 2024. https://www.britannica.com/biography/Fritz-Pollard.

Evans, Farrell. "Fritz Pollard Fought for Racial Equality in the NFL." *NBC News*. September 11, 2019. https://www.nbcnews.com/news/nbcblk/fritz-pollard-african-american-founding-father-nfl-n1052046.

"Fritz Pollard's Enshrinement Speech Transcript | Pro Football Hall of Fame." Pro Football Hall of Fame. January 1, 2005. https://www.profootballhof.com/news/2005/01/news-fritz-pollard-s-enshrinement-speech-transcript.

Ohemena, Afia. "The Forgotten Pollards—Rogers Park/West Ridge Historical Society." Rogers Park/West Ridge Historical Society. May 25, 2019. https://rpwrhs.org/2014/07/28/the-forgotten-pollards.

Smith, Ronald A, and John M. Carroll. "Fritz Pollard: Pioneer in Racial Advancement." *The Journal of American History* 79, no. 4 (March 1, 1993): 1655. https://doi.org/10.2307/2080318.

Waleik, Gary. "Fritz Pollard: The Small Running Back Who Broke Big Barriers | Only a Game." WBUR. January 12, 2018. https://www.wbur.org/onlyagame/2018/01/12/fritz-pollard-football.

CHAPTER 5: GYMNASTICS

SIMONE BILES

Aten, Jason. "Simone Biles's 12-Word Response to the Possibility of Not Making the Olympics Is One of the Best Examples of Emotional Intelligence I've Seen." *Inc.* January 29, 2024. https://www.inc.com/jason-aten/simone-biles-12-word-response-to-not-making-olympics-is-best-example-of-emotional-intelligence-ive-seen-yet.html.

Biles, Simone. *Courage to Soar: A Body in Motion, A Life In Balance.* Grand Rapids, MI: Zondervan, 2018.

Bregman, Scott. "Simone Biles' Bravest Act: Choosing Herself." *Olympics.* February 4, 2022. https://olympics.com/en/news/simone-biles-bravest-act-choosing-herself.

Britannica, s.v. "Simone Biles." Accessed December 22, 2023. https://www.britannica.com/biography/Simone-Biles.

Gunston, Jo. "Simone Biles: All Titles, Records and Medals—Complete List." *Olympics.* October 8, 2023. https://olympics.com/en/news /simone-biles-all-titles-records-medals-complete-list.

Hahn, Jason. "Simone Biles 'Slept All the Time' after Larry Nassar Sexual Abuse: 'My Way to Escape Reality.'" *People Magazine.* July 6, 2021. https://people.com/sports/simone-biles-open-up-about-suffering -sexual-abuse.

Legatt, Aviva. "Why Simone Biles Chose an Online College over UCLA." *Forbes.* April 3, 2018. https://www.forbes.com/sites/avivalegatt /2018/04/03/why-simone-biles-chose-online-over-ucla /?sh=1706bb983193.

Park/Tokyo, Alice. "These Are All the Gymnastics Moves Named after Simone Biles." *TIME.* July 26, 2021. https://time.com/6083539 /gymnastics-moves-named-after-simone-biles.

Scahd, Tom. "Simone Biles Wins 2023 U.S. Classic during Return to Competitive Gymnastics." *USA TODAY.* Last updated August 6, 2023. https://www.usatoday.com/story/sports/olympics/2023/08/05/simone -biles-live-updates-return-competitive-gymnastics-2023-us-classic /70531328007.

"What More Can I Say? | Simone Biles Is Known as a Four Time Olympic . . ." Facebook. July 6, 2021. https://www.facebook.com/vsonwatch /videos/234761905126834.

DOMINIQUE DAWES

Britt, Donna. "Growing For the Gold." *Washington Post.* January 7, 2024. https://www.washingtonpost.com/archive/local/1996/07/19/growing -for-the-gold/e360c1c8-49ea-4d09-8e2d-d041cf90923d.

Cale Clarke—The Faith Explained Institute. "My Conversation with Olympic Gold Medalist Dominique Dawes." YouTube. July 23, 2021. https://www.youtube.com/watch?v=hkxfCDKevvY.

Carter, Dana. "Dominique Dawes, Hello My Name Is Dana Podcast Interview." YouTube. August 5, 2022. https://www.youtube.com /watch?v=jhnhhDkskE8.

"Dominique Dawes." *Olympics.* Accessed March 18, 2024. https://olympics.com/en/athletes/dominique-dawes.

"Dominique Dawes." The International Gymnastics Hall of Fame. Accessed March 18, 2024. https://www.ighof.com/inductees/2009 _Dominique_Dawes.php.

"Dominique Dawes' Hair Story—'I Am Finally Natural!'" Curly Nikki. September 10, 2021. https://www.curlynikki.com/2012/08/dominique -dawes-hair-story-i-am-finally.html.

Frey, Jennifer. "Not Too Old for Games." *Washington Post.* June 25, 1996. https://www.washingtonpost.com/wp-srv/sports/olympics/daily /june/28/notold.htm.

Glauber, Bill. "Vaulting onto the Olympics Stage Marylander's Career Began at McDonald's." *Baltimore Sun.* October 25, 2018. https://www.baltimoresun.com/1992/05/31/vaulting-onto-the-olympic -stage-marylanders-career-began-at-mcdonalds.

Goldberg, Natalie Rose. "Four-Time Olympic Medalist Dominique Dawes on How She Defines Success." CNBC. August 3, 2023. https://www.cnbc .com/2023/08/03/four-time-olympic-medalist-dominique-dawes-on -how-she-defines-success.html.

Mattingly, Diane. "Dawes Has Many Moves, Only One Destination." *Washington Post.* January 2, 2024. https://www.washingtonpost.com /archive/sports/1991/06/30/dawes-has-many-moves-only-one -destination/1aaf0775-cf7c-44af-a34b-84a6aa46fcbd.

Preston, Mike. "Dawes' Golden Life Has Few Free Moments GYMNASTICS." *Baltimore Sun.* October 24, 2018. https://www .baltimoresun.com/1994/10/15/dawes-golden-life-has-few-free -moments-gymnastics.

Staff, "Dawes Hoping for Spot on 2000 Olympic Team." *Buffalo News.* May 24, 2000. https://buffalonews.com/news/dawes-hoping-for-spot -on-2000-olympic-team/article_d578f00e-c4f9-536c-8198 -dfbdaf12c3cd.html.

The Welcome Conference. "Dominique Dawes—Success Is a Journey, not a Destination." YouTube. October 17, 2023. https://www.youtube.com /watch?v=FYwqdO-C4Lk.

CHAPTER 6: TRACK AND FIELD

ALLYSON FELIX

"Allyson Felix." United States Olympic and Paralympic Committee. Accessed March 18, 2024. https://www.teamusa.com/profiles/allyson -felix-807126.

"Allyson Felix Retires from Track Career That Brought Joy, Heartbreak —NBC Sports." *NBC Sports.* July 15, 2022. https://www.nbcsports .com/olympics/news/allyson-felix-retire-track-and-field-world -championships.

Britannica, s.v. "Allyson Felix." Accessed December 29, 2023. https://www.britannica.com/biography/Allyson-Felix.

Felix, Allyson. "Always There by Allyson Felix | The Players' Tribune." The Players' Tribune. August 6, 2021. https://www.theplayerstribune.com /articles/allyson-felix-olympics-brother.

Felix, Allyson, Lindsay Crouse, Taige Jensen, and Max Cantor. "Opinion | Allyson Felix: My Own Nike Pregnancy Story." *The New York Times.* January 3, 2020. https://www.nytimes.com/2019/05/22/opinion/allyson -felix-pregnancy-nike.html.

Hashemzadeh, Kianoosh. "Allyson Felix Is Not Done." USC Rossier. March 29, 2023. https://rossier.usc.edu/news-insights/news/allyson-felix -not-done.

Layden, Tim. "Catch Her if You Can: California Sprinter Allyson Felix will Soon be Giving Marion Jones a Run for Her Money." *Sports Illustrated.* June 9, 2003. https://vault.si.com/vault/2003/06/09/catch-her -if-you-can-california-sprinter-allyson-felix-will-soon-be-giving-marion -jones-a-run-for-her-money.

"Taken for Granted: Allyson Felix on Defeating Disappointment and Savoring Success (Transcript)." TED. October 19, 2021. https://www.ted .com/podcasts/worklife/taken-for-granted-allyson-felix-on-defeating -disappointment-and-savoring-success-transcript.

Trevelyan, Mark, and Mike Collett-White. "U.S. Reigns on Track and Beach." *Reuters.* August 8, 2012. https://www.reuters.com/article/us-oly -wrap-day12-idUSBRE87702H20120808.

Verma, Shreya. "'Had the Nickname Chicken Legs': US Olympic Legend Allyson Felix Reveals How She Was Bullied as a Student for Being Too

Thin." EssentiallySports. January 20, 2022. https://www.essentiallysports.com/us-sports-news-athletics-news-had-the-nickname-chicken-legs-us-olympic-legend-allyson-felix-reveals-how-she-was-bullied-as-a-student-for-being-too-thin.

Weir, Stuart. "28 Questions to Allyson Felix, from the *RunBlogRun* Archives." *RunBlogRun*. October 21, 2022. https://www.runblogrun.com/2022/10/28-questions-to-allyson-felix-december-2018-from-the-runblogrun-archives.html.

ALICE COACHMAN

"Alice Coachman, 90, Dies; First Black Woman to Win Olympic Gold." *The New York Times*. July 15, 2014. https://www.nytimes.com/2014/07/15/sports/alice-coachman-90-dies-groundbreaking-medalist.html.

"Alice Coachman, Who Won a Gold Medal but Came Home to Segregation." *The New York Times*. August 19, 2016. https://www.nytimes.com/interactive/projects/cp/obituaries/archives/alice-coachman.

Britannica, s.v. "Alice Coachman." Accessed January 24, 2024. https://www.britannica.com/biography/Alice-Coachman.

Greenblatt, Alan. "Why an African-American Sports Pioneer Remains Obscure." NPR. July 19, 2014. https://www.npr.org/sections/codeswitch/2014/07/19/332665921/why-an-african-american-sports-pioneer-remains-obscure.

Miles Educational Film Productions. "Interview with Alice Coachman." Washington University in St. Louis. Last accessed June 18, 2024. http://repository.wustl.edu/concern/videos/b27740880.

Phelps, Shirelle, and Gale Research Inc. *Contemporary Black Biography, V18: Profiles from the International Black Community*. Detroit, MI: Gale, 1998.

"USA Track & Field | Alice Coachman." USATF. Accessed March 18, 2024. https://www.usatf.org/athlete-bios/alice-coachman.

VisionaryProject. "Alice Coachman: I Wanted to Be Famous." YouTube. March 31, 2010. https://www.youtube.com/watch?v=By_Po8wzn1M.

VisionaryProject. "Alice Coachman: 'I Was Champ.'" YouTube. March 31, 2010. https://www.youtube.com/watch?v=9fyXAiyywDU.

VisionaryProject. "Alice Coachman: My Time at Tuskegee." YouTube. March 25, 2010. https://www.youtube.com/watch?v=mRYu8HA_ne4.

VisionaryProject. "Alice Coachman: Running Track as a Kid." YouTube. March 25, 2010. https://www.youtube.com/watch?v=iFL0B_P1HGA.

VisionaryProject. "Alice Coachman: A Segregated Homecoming." YouTube. March 31, 2010. https://www.youtube.com/watch?v=YGMG6yzpSk8.

VisionaryProject. "Alice Coachman: Winning the Gold Metal." YouTube, March 31, 2010. https://www.youtube.com/watch?v=iSSt3O9iXHs.

ACKNOWLEDGMENTS

I'd like to thank my family for supporting me through the writing of this book. Your love encourages and inspires me.

I am deeply grateful to Ulysses Press for entrusting me with the opportunity to write about a topic close to my heart: Black history. I also extend my thanks to the editors who diligently worked on the book's production, turning my vision into reality.

This book wouldn't be possible without the inspiration from the sports legends featured within these pages. To the many Black athletes who paved the way and to the many more who follow in those footsteps, thank you for your contributions to history, sport, and Black excellence.

Lastly, I'd like to thank my young achievers for reading this book. I hope these stories motivate you to aim high and achieve your goals.

ABOUT THE AUTHOR

Sophia Murphy is a freelance writer based in Toronto, Canada. She is an avid reader who loves detective mysteries and superhero movies. When she's not writing or reading, you can find her singing along to her favorite songs or in a fierce board game competition with her husband and two boys. *Sports Superstars from Black History* is her first trivia book for kids. Sophia is excited to follow her writing dreams, wherever they take her.